D0491615

The
Denigration
of Capitalism

The Denigration of Capitalism
Six Points of View

Michael Novak, editor

David B. Burrell, C.S.C.
Bernard Cooke
Martin E. Marty
Edward R. Norman
James V. Schall, S.J.

American Enterprise Institute for Public Policy Research
Washington, D.C.

Cover illustration by Karen Laub-Novak.

Library of Congress Cataloging in Publication Data

Main entry under title:

The Denigration of capitalism.

  (AEI studies ; 261)
  CONTENTS: Novak, M. Introduction.—Norman, E. R. Denigration of
capitalism: current education and the moral subversion of capitalist
society.—Marty, M. E. On Black, White, Gray, and the rainbow.—[etc.]
  1. Christianity and capitalism—Addresses, essays, lectures. I. Novak,
Michael. II. Burrell, David B. III. Series: American Enterprise Institute
for Public Policy Research. AEI studies ; 261.
BR115.C3D46   261.8'5   79-23650
ISBN 0-8447-3364-4

AEI Studies 261

Printed in the United States of America

CONTENTS

Introduction

Michael Novak

A number of years ago, the distinguished British scientist and novelist C. P. Snow observed that a main theme of British literature for two centuries had been antimodern, antimachine, "Luddite." Although Snow emphasized only the extent to which the animus of the literary tradition—from William Blake's "dark satanic mills" to Evelyn Waugh's scathing satires—was directed against the machine, it was also directed, and more basically, against the rise of a commercial and bourgeois civilization.

During the winter of 1978–1979, I was reading extensively in the criticism of capitalism. Why, I asked myself, is the anti-capitalist animus so strong, across so many intellectual disciplines?

Humanists, poets, and artists may be forgiven, of course, for preferring the status they held under the dukes, princes, and crowns of the aristocratic age. Moral and aesthetic terms—for instance, calling someone "noble" or a "prince" of a man—once also invoked class and station. The struggle for survival and the aspiration to improve one's station seemed in feudal times inferior to moral and aesthetic considerations. In those days, to labor, to be frugal, to manage one's worldly enterprises as a good steward, and so to prosper, were acts full of religious and human meaning. The larger over-arching meanings of life were considered most important. To focus too intently upon the economic side of life, to concentrate central energies upon it, was disdained both by religious and by humanistic standards as vulgar and self-deforming.

How shocking, then, was the rise of the commercial and industrial spirit. This spirit had three parts. It arose, first, in the revolutionary perception that the wealth of nations is not fixed but subject to immense, even unimaginable increase. It argued, second, that a greater

1

application of practical intelligence might vastly enlarge the output of human industry. Finally, it recognized that personal incentives are the great driving force of human consciousness and could tame the human race to civilizing, wealth-producing, peaceable pursuits.

This new spirit was antiheroic, even antiromantic. It thought to turn even the will-to-power from military to economic adventure, from political to commercial enterprise. Whereas the feudal age had been built around secular themes, like station and status, the new age of democratic capitalism would be built around the secular rights, incentives, and ambitions of individuals. For religious thinkers, this transvaluation of values was traumatic. Often described as a transition from religious to secular consciousness—as "secularization"—it was, in fact, a shift from one secular order to another. It was a shift, however, from an order ancient, familiar, and long assimilated into religious sensibility to an order novel, threatening, and ominous.

For artists and for intellectuals of any age, the commercial marketplace is not a satisfactory measure of intrinsic value. The better an artist, the smaller may be the audience that, at least at first, appreciates the originality of his vision and technique. Commercial acclaim may fall upon a life's work only long after the artist's death. As the aristocratic patrons of the arts and intellect lost status in the rising democratic capitalist age, so also did aristocratic tastes and standards. Artists and intellectuals, quite naturally, experienced a sense of loss. Many came to loathe the "philistine" culture that began to replace the aristocratic and religious culture which had so highly valued their work in better days.

I was studying such matters in 1978–1979 because I was restless under the prejudices in which I had been reared. It seemed to me that the conceptual schemes in my head were out of tune with the evidence of my senses. As a theologian, I recognized that no generation of theologians before my own had ever been so thoroughly favored by the economics, politics, and cultural values of the system in which they lived. There are now tens of thousands of scholars in religion, free to travel and to converse, well supplied with libraries, books, and personal facilities. The entire planet lies within our range of study and is open to our access. Have ever Christian theologians been so favored?

When I turned to books like Michael Harrington's *Twilight of Capitalism*,[1] I was struck by how empty were the Marxist categories and sympathies in which I had been educated. First, the category of

---

[1] Michael Harrington, *The Twilight of Capitalism* (New York: Simon and Schuster, 1976).

"alienation," which I had once found meaningful, struck me as inauthentic and false, based as it is upon a nostalgia for a mythic world of wholeness that never was. I know enough about medieval serfs not to believe that their own hard and honest labor had been "un-alienated." Were not my grandparents exactly serfs, right into the twentieth century in Slovakia, where they had been kept in forced ignorance, without civil rights, unable to own their own property? Their migration from a feudal into a democratic capitalist system gives the lie to nostalgia.

Second, even supposing that I accept Harrington's picture of Marx as a democratic socialist, open, empirical of temper, passionately committed to a "whole" and "organic" vision of society, a kind of Edmund Burke of the East, I have become skeptical of "organic" theories of society, whether enunciated by conservatives or by revolutionaries. I am skeptical because, as logic dictates and as my eyes can see, the effort to impose "humane" and "organic" values upon the whole of society is inevitably authoritarian and, when extended to the life of the spirit, totalitarian. It is so because individuals do not all share the same values or desire the same things. With Marx, Harrington loathes the "substantive irrationalities" of the democratic capitalist marketplace. In his eyes, it is wrong that the prostitute may be rewarded in the marketplace, while desperately needed housing for poor families, unable to afford what they need, may never be built. And yet, in real life, millions of persons in the United States live in nonprofit housing. So I wonder who, in Harrington's world, will decide what is "rational." If the decision is made democratically in our society, it will be made through some instrument that organizes 220 million individual decisions, exactly the role imperfectly played now by our democratic politics and multiple markets. If the decision is made by experts who disagree with our own values and preferences, we will certainly not describe their decisions as "substantively rational." To seek a social organization that is "substantively rational" is an exercise of yet another form of nostalgia. Given the pluralism and multiplicity of free human agents, no imposition of rationality from above serves liberty, and no imposition from below (by most or all agents choosing the same things) is likely to meet the standards of dissidents.

Third, in the details of the Marxist case against democratic capitalism, every sort of counterargument springs to mind. Marx did not perceive clearly enough the real power of the democratic component of democratic capitalism. This component led to modifications of the system that permitted many workers to live better than had the aristocrats of preceding generations and permitted the children of workers such mobility that no station or profession of life would be closed to them. Marx argues that the worker who agrees to work for four dollars an hour when his output earns six dollars is cheated of the "surplus value" of two dollars, and is paid only two-thirds of what his labor is worth. But someone else must invest in the ideas, machinery, and system of distribution and marketing that make the enterprise a financial success. Laboring all alone, with their own two hands, the laborers might not be able to earn anything close to four dollars an hour. Thus, for them there are incentives to risk employment at that rate. For others, there are incentives to risk their investments in enterprises that might employ many laborers, when they might instead spend their money on castles, yachts, and expensive parties, imitating the idle rich of yore. Business organizations, even many large ones, often fail to bring in enough money to pay their laborers the agreed-upon hourly rate. There are workers whose output is a "deficit value."

Perhaps these notes are enough to suggest how I was beginning to question the biases I had been educated in: biases according to which business corporations are the enemy of humanism and human welfare. It is not easy to keep believing that at the root of human ills in our world lie the profit motive and the market. I was taught that "public" describes virtuous, selfless, noble efforts concerned for the common good, whereas "private" describes selfish, greedy, irrational efforts. But I could hardly help noting that public enterprises had their own corruptions and irrationalities. I was brought up in that part of Democratic liberalism (I was a speech writer for George McGovern in 1972) which was mildly socialist; which looked to the extension of the power of the federal government as the main instrument by which to "humanize" and "rationalize" our system. I had willingly joined—and still now belong to—the social democratic movement, linked to the League for Industrial Democracy and its publication, *New America*. What is new is my willingness to be as critical of the left as I ever was of the right, and to examine the history and theory of democratic capitalism with fresh eyes. Certainly, democratic capitalism needs criticism. But I no longer believe that socialism offers the best perspective—"the pervasive light" as Michael Harrington puts it—for a penetrating criticism of our system. Quite to the contrary. I consider socialism worse than the system it would heal, and its assumptions erroneous in theory and full of fatal contradictions in practice. Socialism is a mystification. There must be a better set of ideals.

4

It was in this context that a friend sent me a copy of Edward Norman's lecture "Denigration of Capitalism." That essay indicated that other theologians besides myself, coming from a viewpoint like my own, were reconsidering the prejudices of their own minds. As I have been a lifelong Democrat, so Dr. Norman has been a partisan of the Labour Party in Great Britain. Yet as a historian, he could not help noting a rather grotesque bias in the intellectual history of the last two hundred years, a bias which Lionel Trilling has called one of the most remarkable phenomena in all of human history: the adversarial bent of virtually an entire intellectual elite against its own culture.

What sort of self-hatred is involved in our own hearts? What is the history of our own paradigms, conceptual schemes, mental blinders, as we try to understand the actual conditions of our lives? I determined to invite several other theologians to comment on Dr. Norman's theme. It is obvious from this account that I had my own way of reading Dr. Norman's lecture, reprinted here in its original form. The other commentators in this volume read it rather differently. My original hopes were that the full discussion would illustrate better than any other volume how a representative group of Christian theologians thinks about the very general question Dr. Norman introduces, that a discussion would be opened, and that stepping stones would be planted toward future work in many directions. Those intentions have been filled beyond my expectations.

More and more, the Christian churches—whether in papal discourses or in studies produced by the World Council of Churches—are turning their attention to economics. No one can plausibly hold that the theology of economic systems is one of the better developed branches of Christian inquiry. The world now lies before us full of empirical evidence about the workings of various sorts of capitalist and socialist systems during the past forty years. Regrettably, many theological inquiries into these matters have been conducted as though this evidence did not demand new premises, new concepts, new types of inquiries. As will be seen from the discussions that follow, each of the participants in this symposium felt the urgency of further conceptual work.

It remains to thank Dr. Norman for stimulating the discussion on this side of the Atlantic, to express appreciation to the contributors for their good work, and to commend John W. Cooper, a graduate student of religion at Syracuse University and now my research assistant, for his editorial help.

Professor D. B. Robertson of Syracuse University, the distinguished Niebuhr scholar, provided a great fund of research notes on

Reinhold Niebuhr's lifelong struggle with socialism and his growing appreciation for democratic capitalism; but his schedule did not permit him, this early, to summarize his research in this volume, as I had hoped.

This publication is the fourth in a series of publications on religion and public policy published by the American Enterprise Institute. We hope through future publications to stimulate further questions for research and many fruitful arguments.

September 1979

Denigration of Capitalism

Current Education and the Moral Subversion of Capitalist Society

Edward R. Norman

I do not need to say that capitalism lacks influential intellectual exponents in our day. It is regarded by some as a regrettable necessity; by others as an inheritance from the past which the moral sense of mankind has already rejected but which requires some remaining practical steps to remove its baneful consequences; and by some others as inevitably doomed through its own internal contradictions— a system both corrupting to its beneficiaries and destructive of the personalities of the labouring masses. The idealism of the young is largely turned against it. Educated opinion in general is full of moral censoriousness about the supposed debasing consequences of capitalism for the human spirit. Consider the number of influential and prestigious publications each year which either favour collectivist economic or social arrangements, or which, through moralistic condemnation of the effects of capitalism, undermine its claim to be regarded as an enlightened or a proper manner of conducting economic relationships in society. I was recently talking to someone just returned from the east, where, he said, the young simply could not lay hands on any books or literature about economic or social issues which were not deeply critical of capitalism. He asked if I could name a few titles, easily available in the West, which could be suggested as correctives. There are very few to suggest: yet go into any bookshop in London, and there you will see rows of works about society and the economy which assume the superiority of collectivist or socialist systems.

One of the assumptions of the prevailing outlook is that capitalism may arguably have some practical advantages, but that it has no theoretical justification—it is a crude survivor from the harsh dynamism of the entrepreneurial spirit of the nineteenth century, an *ad hoc*

7

device for the rapid but irresponsible creation of wealth. It is, as it seems, so crude that it is amazing it has survived at all, and in the developing countries, unencumbered with an industrial past, few are found to advocate it as a meritorious system in its own right. Those critics who speak of the resilience of capitalism attribute it not to inherent proved advantages, but to the powerful control, exercised to preserve the economic and social *status quo*, by capitalists themselves. And by "capitalists," of course, they do not mean the small investors, the pension funds, or the holdings of the Trades Unions: they mean the caricature depictures of cigar-smoking men in expensive motor-cars—the staple matter, not only of the social vision of such as the Soviet satirical magazine *Krokodil*, but also of numerous BBC documentaries and dramas.

The overwhelming view offered in the available authorities, therefore, presents capitalism as notably lacking moral dimensions. It is a strange reversal of the position of a century-and-a-half ago, when capitalism was promoted by the high-minded and the moralists of that period precisely because of its moral qualities. Some of their ideals are no longer appropriate to our society, but some others urgently need to be rescued from the oblivion to which they are sinking. For the morality of capitalism has first to do with the morality of choice; with the individual's freedom to select, either as producer or consumer, from among alternative sources of economic enterprise. It is the freedom left to the individual to have a control over his own labour: the direct contradiction of the Marxist assertion that a man alienates his freedom and his personality by selling his labour to another. Provided the conditions of work are adequately safeguarded, on both sides equally, at law, the risks are the same for the man whose effort is rendered in organisational skills, and who chances his enterprise or his capital, as they are for the man who sells his labour. The unequal distribution of wealth which follows has attracted severe condemnation: noticeably from those academic and ecclesiastical observers who are most obviously its beneficiaries. But it is a minor feature of a much larger and more beneficial result: the maintenance of the means of livelihood independently of the state—an essential condition in a society where there is no agreement among those concerned with social organisation about what the ethical basis of the state should be.

There is another feature of capitalism even less appealing to the contemporary social outlook than the practice of economic choice: the relationship between enterprise and personal moral character. It is true that the competitive element in capitalism has some disagreeable

8

side-effects which the moral sense of men will contain. Mr. Heath once spoke wisely of the "unacceptable face" of some sorts of enterprise, and he was right to do so. Selfish disregard of social unfortunates has always been one pit into which some have fallen: another has been the separation of so-called business ethics from private morality. But these are errors which, again, do no justice to the greater moral advantages of the competitive principle. For these advantages are—in the now discredited expression—"character forming." The competitive deployment of personal resources and talents is a tremendous stimulus to moral self-consciousness; it encourages, rather than discourages, the individual in the cultivation of a practical scheme of responsibility for his actions, and imposes, as a condition of maintaining living standards, a sense of moral duty. This is usually lacking in a society where the state acts for the individual in matters of social responsibility—in a society with an underdeveloped sense of national moral identity: a society like our own today. Then there is a danger far worse than the abuses to which the competitive ethos gives rise: there is a massive social relapse into moral indigence —a leading feature today, when opinion dwells obsessively on social morality but says little about the personal moral worth of the individuals who compose society. It regards a social conscience in a man as an indication of moral excellence—an assumption, to which I shall return later, which is open to question from several perspectives.

Capitalism is also characterized by a recognition of the supervening fact of individual self-interest. It is, to that extent, realistic about human nature. It is candid about men's self-seeking priorities, and tries to harness their energies to the creation of wealth, in the belief that increased wealth will benefit the whole of society. Morality requires self-interest to become "enlightened": that is to say, the productive use of personal resources in the creation of wealth will itself suggest the context for the exercise of moral considerations in social relationships, rather than on pre-determined blueprints of economic morality, enforced by the rule of law, fashioned by those who have arrived at what they think is best for everyone, and unvarying in its application in a real world where men are enormously diverse in their moral sense and personal responsibility. The reverse of capitalism's realism about men is the optimistic view of human nature embodied in most formulations of liberalism. Historically—in the nineteenth century—capitalism, expressed in laissez faire practice, and liberalism, went hand in hand. But they were full of contradictions; and the self-interest basis of the capitalist ethic, once it had become obviously incompatible with the abstract notions about humanity implicit in the liberals' view of man, laid itself open to assault from its former partner. Perhaps it can even be said that modern social democracy is the resulting version of liberalism minus capitalism. The good intentions of modern social collectivists, of whatever brand, always come to wreck upon their false optimism about human nature. For men do not naturally act in the interests of their fellows. They need the ultimate sanctions of religion for that, or, more materially, the coercion of the economic need to labour, and the prospect of self-improvement, to overcome the vicious consequences to which their self-seeking impulses are otherwise liable to proceed. This pessimism about human nature was once universal. It was the central core of the Christian doctrine of Original Sin. It lay at the root of nearly all serious political theorizing until a century or so ago. It emphasised the utility of civil government as a means of curbing the corrupt state of nature into which men fall once artificial restraints upon their self-seeking instincts are abandoned. And the obligation of labour was the sort of restraint which many theorists regarded as most essential for the creation of moral social responsibility. Without individual choice in the matter of labour, however, and the "enlightened" channelling of self-interest that resulted, individuals were thought incapable of freedom. Astonishingly, today, this body of traditional moral attitudes is scarcely mentioned. The model man of the twentieth century is a creature of autonomous reason, able to calculate and to control the consequences of his impulses, characterized by a degree of altruism—if educated the right way, that is—and, once liberated from the evil effects of social injustices, given to abstract love of humanity. This model is the orthodoxy of social planners and radical political idealists. Where they see men acting as they have always acted, and always will—selfishly—they look around to find some social agency, some class in society, some environmental condition, which has sullied the pure waters of human benevolence. "Capitalism" is the source of men's fallen state: that is the conventional response of our own social democracy, just as much as it is of the Marxists in their critique of human life.

But capitalism aspires to the realisation of an enlightened self-interest; to educate men into a more rational social state, by the productive use of their selfish instincts. That is its moral purpose. It accepts men as they are, and turns their instincts to the beneficial practices of personal and productive industry. That is the moral purpose which is now familiarly caricatured—as everything about capitalism is—in the crude depictures of Victorian exhortations to hard work as a device to establish moral and class authoritarianism.

There is another moral dimension to capitalism, also now neglected in public discussion. Because capitalism is pessimistic about men and their instincts, it is suspicious of blanket social coercion. It promotes private enterprise as a means of preserving freedom—by *not* obliging others to subscribe to an ideology necessarily attached to the means of economic production (as Marxism does), or to a social morality prescribed by élite opinion in the state (as liberalism now does). There are, of course, some practical reductions in the area of ideological selection that may have to be made in capitalist society—at least as far as collective concepts go—but they are in the end seen to be negligible, from the point of view of preserving freedom, compared with the flattening effects of the arrangements imposed by the coercive jurisdiction of the collectivist state. This is especially true when these impositions are made, as they always are, in the name of social morality. The prescription of an economic framework by a relatively small number of large capitalists in a society of mixed social and political attitudes presents a much more manoeuverable situation, and allows a greater possibility of personal freedom to the citizens, than the enforcement by legal compulsion of the moral opinions of the élite who define the issues which direct the policies of both totalitarian collectivisms and social democracies.

These are the simple outlines of the morality of capitalism. Each feature, of course, is modified in experience, and to that extent removed from a systematic or ideal model. And it is, as a matter of fact, one of the most advantageous features of capitalism that is *not* a systematic and rationalized ideology or structure. The price to pay for that is a lot of loose ends, and the obloquy of the rationalist-minded theorists. Capitalism is full of minor evils, existing beneath the umbrella of its overall good effect of preserving individual freedom. I am not seeking to establish a case for a completely uncontrolled market economy, in an actual or a moral sense. The minor evils of capitalist society clearly need the attention of legislative restraint and charitable palliatives. There are areas where the intervention of the state is required to provide welfare or public utilities which are not the appropriate functions of private enterprise. Such practical modifications correspond to experience and reality. The trouble is that they tend to get out of hand. In our day, there is a great need to preserve the balance, because inroads upon the centre of capitalist freedom are now made, more than ever, in the name of a compelling social moral conscience. The contemporary assault upon capitalism—to which I shall now turn—is very moralistic in exactly this sense.

11

The philosophical attack upon capitalism is open and clear. Though not by any means confined to Marxism, it is Marxist doctrine which, in our own times, most appeals to enemies of capitalism. My purpose today is to explore the less open, less clear forces ranged against capitalism: Marxism identifies itself and can be met on the various levels it selects. I will, however, make one observation about it, because there is one particular Marxist doctrine which, if true, would do considerable damage to what I have been suggesting about capitalism's rôle as the preserver of individual freedom. Marxists contend that in capitalist society people are incapable of real choice because they have their options and attitudes pre-selected for them by the consequences of a controlled education, culture, and economic environment. Marxists call this condition one of "false consciousness": its victims are incapable of realising that their known will is different from what they would *really* will if the options were differently presented. Similarly, Marxists argue that liberty in capitalist society is reduced in practice to a number of so-called formal freedoms. This means that the apparent legal right to act as a free agent is in practice negated by a denial of the means of putting the right into operation. Here is a homely illustration once offered by the Very Revd. Dr. Hewlett Johnson, "Red" Dean of Canterbury:

> Permission and opportunity stand poles apart. The labourer
> has "formal" freedom to smoke cigars. Being poor, he lacks
> the opportunity; the "formal" permission is useless. In the
> matter of cigars he lacks freedom. Formal permission avails
> him not at all. And so it is throughout the whole of society.

The Dean's analysis has, in effect, been overtaken by events, as anyone will know who has visited a working men's club or been to the Spanish coast in the summer. Yet it must be conceded that the concepts of "false consciousness" and "formal freedom" are serious sociological observations. The trouble is, from the Marxists' point of view, that they are universally applicable, being attached not by chance, but by necessity, to all social conditions. They are, indeed, in our own day, much more obviously in evidence in socialist countries than they are in the Western democracies. Few, surely, can imagine the Soviet citizen luxuriating in choice as to the moral or economic alternatives presented to him; or that the millions of Cambodians or South Vietnamese who have been expelled from their cities and herded into rural labour camps are the beneficiaries of actual rather than "formal" freedom. Nor are these two instances just regrettable lapses from a normal ideological purity, as some

British and American Marxists argue, as they behold the monstrous tyrannies conducted in their name throughout the world. For societies are always run by élites. Our own is; so are the socialist totalitarian states. Most countries today are run by *educated* élites, rather than by those who owe their authority to family inheritance or princely *diktat*. No doubt the priority of élites is necessary, in order to move society to some higher purpose, or to prevent a cruder version of demagogy, or simply because the educated always float to the top by the unfailing attractiveness of their high-minded sponsorship of moralistic principles. But whatever the mechanics, the crucial matter is still *choice*: the ability to change the élite if they are challenged by another section of élitist opinion—which is the most common form of all political change, especially in revolutionary situations— or if the élite is too far removed from the common assumptions of what is right and just in a society where popular opposition stands a chance of organising the vote. It is in capitalist societies that choice in this (admittedly restricted) sense still operates with the fewest encumbrances. It certainly operates within the limitations of "false consciousness" and "formal freedom," but it is very much more flexible in the crucial areas of choice than alternative social and economic arrangements have so far shown themselves to be. Perhaps, in fact, in the longest perspective, Europe and North America in the nineteenth and twentieth centuries will prove to have been the one time in human development when a serious attempt was made to allow effectively free institutions. Already the area of freedom in the sense we have attempted is rapidly diminishing, as nation after nation falls to the old tyrannies of the new controlled societies. Perhaps we shall have been no more than a brief and only too imperfect interlude, an odd departure from the normal condition of mankind.

In our society, Marxism is not widespread, however much it may have acquired acceptance among small groups of intellectuals and trade unionists. The threat to capitalism here comes from much more conventional and respectable "establishment" thinking. Many who would be surprised to be told that their attitudes and principles were operating against the survival of capitalism are *in fact* ranged against it. The intellectual fashions of the time promote several basic assumptions whose implications are hostile. First among them is the destruction of the moral authority of the past: the growing insistence, in the historical interpretations now commonplace in the schools and universities, that capitalist society has been characterized by class oppression, social injustice, and almost callous indifference by the ruling groups to the conditions of life among the masses. Here are

13

the familiar tableaux of the flint-faced capitalists, the Daumier cartoons of the reeking slums, the vogue for Mayhew's London proletarians, the Chartist hagiography, the rehabilitation of the once-scorned prophets of contemporary practices such as feminism, birth control, and all the other requisites of our present-day sense of moral worth. This view of Victorian England is not exactly mythical, for aspects of nineteenth-century society confirm the existence of living standards which, judged against the scale of modern expectation, were poor indeed. But the qualification about "expectations" is crucial: it is the modern assumption that Victorian society was a nexus of social *deprivation* which is false. If you stand some way back from the much-deplored state of Victorian society—much deplored in its own day, too—a quite different set of perspectives appears. Now immense enterprise can be seen. Here was the fastest growing economy and population the world has ever seen; and, despite some minor fluctuations, the total picture is of an astonishing improvement in the living conditions, the health and wealth, of a whole people—all accomplished within an incredibly short space of time, a little more than a century. It is true that a relatively small number of people became extremely rich; but it is also true that their creation of wealth lifted the living standards of everyone. What a contrast, too, with rural society. Those who moralize about the industrial slums of Victorian Britain should realise that living conditions in them were very much better than in the rural squalor from which the population had voluntarily removed—attracted by the prospects and the realities of improvement. The smoky cities we have been conditioned to loathe were, to Victorian working people, exactly the reverse. They were symbols of a dynamic and progressive new age, offering a new freedom from the deferential closed communities of rural society. The best proof of this sense of liberation was actually the advance of expectations to still better rewards for labour. Downtrodden masses do not, as a rule, make effective material for the generation of popular politics and movements for self-help and education: men whose expectations have already been stimulated by one round of improvements are those who know how to envisage more.

How, then, did we acquire our present dismissive attitudes to the capitalist past? We do not have the Marxists to blame, but our own social reformers and social romantics. The evidence of the appalling state of nineteenth-century society came from the lips of nineteenth-century men themselves. It did not come from neutral and dispassionate observers, however, but from those anxious to create a public conscience over selected social evils. They were active

14

propagandists for change: philanthropists, sanitary experts, medical men and clergy; middle-class men, skilled at influencing the press and packing parliamentary inquiries with witnesses sympathetic to their view of social miseries. Despite their very laudable motives, they unconsciously distorted things, got perspectives and scales wrong; represented, as universal, abuses which were highly restricted in incidence or were anyway just passing away. Britain today is still full of such agents for social improvement; and we know from our experience how, for all the goodness of their passionate concern, they misrepresent the actual state of society—but have ready hearers. To read the propaganda of some contemporary agitations for the homeless or the one-parent families, for example, you would imagine modern Britain to be a sour heap of oppressive social injustice. If such accounts become the historical orthodoxy of the future—which is likely, incidentally—something entirely familiar will have occurred. For the origin of our own view of Victorian society was exactly like that: based upon uncritical acceptance of the propaganda of good but obsessive men pursuing laudable aims. Add to that the rural romanticism, and the antipathy to industrial conditions, which have found so much expression in the Victorian and subsequent literary outpourings of the bourgeois intelligentsia, and you will begin to see why nineteenth-century social conditions have had such a bad press. The literateurs found the working-class men and women they so much pitied very alien; and they proceeded to suppose them alienated. The masses were regarded as victims rather than beneficiaries of the new economic growth. Capitalism was blamed. So was Political Economy, and laissez faire practice: which the agents of change and the literateurs came to regard as merely the systematic application of the class selfishness of the capitalists. Political Economy, however, had been promoted for *moral* reasons. All the progressive forces of the first half of the nineteenth-century advocated it: philosophical radicals, church leaders, legal reformers, and the first rank of politicians of both the major parties. Political Economy was seen not only as creating the conditions in which the multiplication of national wealth could be most effectively fulfilled, from which everyone could benefit, but as guaranteeing individual freedom against the power of the state. They themselves came to discover that some of the devices of Political Economy were the wrong ones, and that some state intervention is always necessary. But as a reasoned attempt to foster better social well-being, in totally uncharted economic waters, the Political Economists' vessel had some merits. Laissez faire was certainly not promoted by entrepreneurs only, but by most enlightened men, who believed it beneficial to the interests of both producers and consumers, of capital and labour. It was favoured by intellectuals; and, in the second half of the nineteenth century, it was other intellectuals (and not the labouring masses) who moved over to kick its authority down, and to find in collectivist practices the vehicle of their new social moralizing.

There is another dimension to the present denigration of capitalist society which enjoys a good deal of prestigious support. It is the body of ideas and assumptions which represents the developing world as being held back through the exploitation of the rich Western nations. This is the centre-piece of the arguments now so often heard in the media and in the schoolroom in favour of a redistribution of the world's wealth. Western capitalism is made the agent of exploitation, as once it served to define the "exploitation" of the industrial masses at home. The two cases have an actual and polemical similarity. In practice the enterprise and expertise of the Western developed nations have begun to lift the living standards of people who, a century or less ago, were sunk in the most appalling thrall of custom and subsistence-living. Just as the enterprise of the few created wealth from which the many benefited in the industrial revolutions of the developed nations, so in the larger world today, the poorer countries are benefiting from economic association with developed economies. What we are seeing is a global escalation of expectations to better standards of material life: those very standards are themselves the invention of the richer nations. This form of "exploitation" has produced some very beneficial results. Consider the living standards of people in Africa today, and compare them with fifty years ago. You have to create wealth before you can distribute it. Are the Western nations to be blamed because the "Third World" countries have not yet made their own economies productive enough to satisfy the expectations so easily raised by politicians speaking about "exploitation" as the reason for their later start in the world's rush to fulfill material desires? There is a compelling case to help the poorer countries for reasons of altruism and benevolence, but not because the capitalist nations have unfairly "exploited" them. There is no peculiar guilt attaching to the earlier development of Europe and North America. To suppose there is—as many do suppose—is to project on a global twentieth-century scale the moralistic criticisms of nineteenth-century capitalism made in the European context. Here are all the familiar ingredients: instead of the downtrodden masses in the slums we now have the peasants in the rice fields; for the flint-faced entrepreneurs we now have the international capitalist monopolies; for the few

16

social idealists with a vision of a new Jerusalem in England's green and pleasant land we now have the directors of Oxfam. The model exactly corresponds. But the issue will almost certainly go by default. Capitalism has long since entered the demonology of the "Third World," and why should it not have done? It is distinguished Western liberal thinkers, just as much as the Marxists, who have taught the poorer nations to regard the demands of Western capitalism as the ultimate cause of their poverty.

Here in Britain, we have another set of attitudes whose general tendency is to sap the moral respectability of capitalism. I mean the prevalence of what may be called "moral collectivism"; it is, in the end, probably the most formidable of the forces ranged against the possibility that young people will regard capitalism as an acceptable economic and social ethic. Our society is now full of people with highly developed social consciences. Social "concern," indeed, is one of the most admired virtues of the age, a sort of secularized sign of grace. People praise youth, because of its eagerness to contend for social justice. It will seem a sort of blasphemy to question it all— but I am going to do so, for two reasons. First, much of the paraded social concern of our day is a bit academic; it has an armchair quality. It has become something of an emotional release for the class guilt of the bourgeois intellectuals and those whom they influence—that enormous number of people who blot up the latest ideas emanating from the fashions of thought set by the pundits of the age and yet who suppose that they are "thinking for themselves." For very many, social concern also expresses an element of class antipathy. For example, most of the subjects which become the content of the social conscience are also ones whose identifiable agents of alleged social injustice can be held up for punitive attention. Landlords, capitalists, unenlightened educationalists, and so forth, are the propaganda caricatures of a great deal of social thinking in our country today. There is a sharp polemical edge to many of the campaigns about housing, race, social welfare—and all the areas in which there is, no doubt, real need for actual concern nevertheless. This aspect of class antipathy is important, and it is conventionally overlooked precisely because it expresses a division of social attitudes between two sections of the same class: the professional class, from whose definitions of social issues and social injustice those lower down the social scale ultimately derive their social moralism. More genuinely altruistic social concern should surely not have this hidden motivation, this concealed punitive element? And it should not make its appeal, as it so often does, by assailing the wealth-producing part of society, the part which will have to finance the inflated conscience of the social moralizers. Hence, incidentally, the great importance of the Duke of Edinburgh's words, published in *The Director* in January—"We have got to come back a little and not concentrate so heavily on the unsuccessful and the unfortunate and the underprivileged, but to create a situation where the enterprising can make their contribution, which will also help the underprivileged." The shrieks of outrage which then arose from the usual sources confirmed the truth of his words.

My second reason for raising queries about the present mode of social concern is allied to the fact that social concern and social criticism go hand in hand today. There are serious political implications. The individuals and pressure groups who agitate social issues inevitably call upon the state, at central and local levels, to finance and sometimes to provide the machinery for the various solutions to social evils. There are a number of possibilities in that which are potentially destructive of freedom. It creates a massive collectivism— the state moving further and further into regulating people's lives, even though with admittedly benevolent intention. This growing state machinery has a reality of its own once in existence (as bureaucracies all do have), and it is all ready to serve the political purposes of less democratic governments, should, at a point in the future, some sort of cataclysmic political change, or a mere slow slide into authoritarian practices, come to pass in this country. Far too much social responsibility is being removed from the area of private moral initiative to the collectivism of the public sector. Political theorists have in the past been much exercised about the problem of whether a moral act loses its virtue if compelled by law. The problem remains an unresolved one in a polity like our own, which does not subscribe to a single moral purpose on behalf of its citizens—as fully collectivist states do. Some have seen the Welfare State as tending that way for its justification: that it removes moral choice by compelling people, through taxation, to provide for others. But I do not believe it is a case in point. For the Welfare State is properly sustained *not* because it embodies some great moral truth about welfare, but because it is an expression of enlightened self-interest. People pay for others in order that they may themselves in time benefit. The moral considerations involved are not systematic or defined. Now the trouble with our society today is that those concerned with social welfare demand ever increasing state action, and state responsibilty, for reasons of public righteousness. That is to say, the new powers are being added to the state in the most harmful way: they are invested with all the dogmatism of agreed moral truths. In the area of economic activity, too, those who argue for an enlarged state rôle tend to do so for moral rather than economic reasons. It amounts to the claim that the state has a superior moral judgment in economic life than those who actually create the wealth. From there, it is a short step to allowing the state a monopoly of *all* morality, the nationalization of everyone's conscience.

In contrast, it could perhaps be said that capitalism represents an economic pluralism which parallels the institutional and ideological pluralism of the Western democracies. It is a scheme which needs some modification, however. Economic rationalizations and consolidations, and the creation of international corporations, have moved capitalism a long way from a simple pluralism. And society, for its part, may not be quite the pluralism which liberal apologists of it suppose either. The idea of a stable pluralism is admittedly an attractive one, in a society like ours, where the ruling élite do not agree about the basic moral foundations. There is in practice a broad consensus about the benefits of representative institutions, about the preservation of certain sorts of individual liberty, and all that sort of thing. But these orthodoxies of democratic liberalism lack an agreed sanction: are they to be taught to children by the state, and enforced on citizens by law, because they are Christian? Or because they are applied Humanism? Or because they are thought to be believed in by a majority? The most crucial areas of moral authority are in practice left undefined; yet the state is accumulating powers of social control and economic regulation in the name of morality. The trouble with the notion of a pluralistic society is that it only works in a society where there is a basic agreement to preserve the pluralism: that means, of course, that sufficient will exists, and enough moral certainty, to condition the population to accept it. But once genuine alternatives appear—as they have done all over the world—the central assumptions about the stability of the pluralism evaporate. There are early-warning signals that that is what is happening in our own society. The moral authority of the individualism which in the past sustained freedom is being sapped by the growing moralism of the advocates of collectivism. The pluralistic society, in fact, may turn out to be nothing other than a society pictured in transition from one set of orthodoxies to another. For historical reasons, a version of capitalism has been the form in which individual freedoms were preserved in our society: we need to be more aware than we are that freedom has no built-in preservatives of its own. Whatever new arrangements follow, if the remnants of capitalist society get swept away, we shall need more effective safeguards to individual liberty than public men at present seem to realise. Otherwise the result will be a species of totalitarianism, however benevolent its face may seem at first.

Another danger arises from the fact that the criticisms of capitalism are usually made in our society by those who have no clear alternative in mind. Unlike the Marxists; that is to say, the social moralizers and liberal opinion are very censorious about the supposed social consequences of capitalism, but less critical about the disagreeable features of alternatives. They are helped in this because at present capitalism is here being replaced by confusion—not by a systematic application of an alternative, as is the case in many other parts of the world. Governments do not help: their practice has been to load private enterprise with restrictions and taxation to the point at which capitalism is rendered nearly incapable of effective function, and then to turn round and say that its performance indicates its failure as an economic system. In both ways, it is capitalism, as such, which gets discredited in the public mind. The Marxists are, once again, having their work of undermining capitalism done for them by the well-intended social reformers of our own society.

To my great regret, I have to add the Christian Churches to the list of those whose social outlook now contributes to the subversion of capitalism. Church leaders are full of the same sort of moralistic criticism of the supposed injustices of capitalism as the rest of the intelligentsia. By singling out particular features, rather than declaring against the whole system, their assault is muted; but their general distaste for the spirit of capitalism is undisguised. Early last year the Archbishop of Canterbury spoke of golden handshakes to retiring industrial directors as "an obscenity." (A few months later, incidentally, in August, the Church of England itself offered a golden handshake of £10,000 to one of its own staff who had resigned from Church House—which, to the evident distress of the Archbishop, was turned down by the man concerned on the grounds that he did not wish to violate his integrity.) In November last year a number of bishops spoke up in favour of the closed shop during a debate on industrial relations in the General Synod of the Church of England. Just before Christmas, the Bishop of Bristol came out with an extraordinary attack upon advertising, as embodying all the deadly sins. It is not clear in what ways those men believe they are qualified to offer these opinions. You may remember that when the bishops tried to intervene in the Coal Strike in 1926, openly on the side of the strikers, Baldwin likened their actions to an attempt by the FBI to bring about a revision of the Athanasian Creed. Some of you may feel moved to a comparable observation. In fact, of course, the bishops are merely responding, in Pavlovian fashion, to the moralistic distaste for private enterprise which now afflicts the bourgeois intelligentsia. But in the world context, too, the Churches are now ranged in support of the enemies of capitalism. Faced with the movements for social revolution in the developing nations of the world, they identify the traditional Christian obligation of concern for the welfare of others with the most skilled Marxist devices to attract liberal and humanitarian consciences to the cause of world revolution. They rationalize all the propaganda rhetoric of the so-called "freedom fighters" as merely the language employed by the oppressed to describe agreed basic truths about human rights. Their enthusiasm for humanity is, in fact, now becoming deeply secularized, despite the theological top-dressing which gets added. The World Council of Churches, I need hardly say, is an international agency well-known for the partisan nature of its judgments and activities. It is an enemy of capitalism; in the long term, it may even prove to have been one of the forces making for the extinction of religion as well as freedom. For the Marxists, when they have eventually profited from the demoralization of capitalism, are likely to have an economical way with the Churches. It is a sad conclusion: the Christian Churches should have been a guardian of the values of individual freedom.

I come at last to the rôle of education. You will, I hope, see at once the relevance of what I have been trying to suggest about the strength and persistence of the attitudes so manifestly undermining the moral authority of capitalism. For the teachers in the schools, and the lecturers in the Universities and Colleges of Education, are notable for their tendency to dwell upon the faults rather than the virtues of capitalist society. Indeed, they are the most pervasive of the agents for disseminating dissatisfaction with existing social values. They will, of course, say that they are teaching the young to be "critical," to acquire an unprejudiced social conscience, to "think for themselves" about the basis of moral and social ideals. They will claim—and doubtless actually believe—that they are preserving a free society by helping others to cultivate the practices of free criticism. Alas, the children are in reality presented not with an open choice, but with endless criticisms of the social and political structure; and by suggesting that all our inherited values are open to question the teachers are destroying the moral authority of the existing social order. In its place, through the device of apparent freedom of critical choice, they indoctrinate the children into a confused social discontent. By repetitive descriptions of the shortcomings of welfare in our society, by frequent reference to social evils, and by attempts to identify the class enemies of enlightened social advance, many teachers present a picture of a society in need of radical change. Capitalism is the first victim of this. All their solutions emphasise more collectivism, rather than the need to foster the creative production of wealth, or the part which ought to be played by individual responsibility. If socialist ideals were subjected to the same sort of hostile scrutiny as capitalist ones are in the classrooms of the land there would be an outcry in Parliament. Of course, there are many exceptions to this general drift, but the main outline of things really cannot be doubted. For a simple illustration, consider the prospects of industrial employment presented to many children in the schools. Working in a factory is not portrayed as a challenging opportunity to stretch themselves in the service of the whole community, as part of a vital team creating the wealth which will make for welfare—a picture, incidentally, often enough used in socialist countries to show the responsibilities and virtues of industrial employment. Instead, factory work is regarded as a third or fourth best: what those do, who are unable to become social workers. Now these fundamentally wrong attitudes are the direct result of the prevailing views about capitalism. The private enterprise of the future does not have a very bright prospect if its work force is demoralized before it even starts.

What is to be done? If the Marxists are right, of course, there is nothing to be done. Capitalism will inexorably collapse inwards when its final great crisis comes. I think you will agree, however, that despite the weight of the forces ranged against it, capitalism's final great crises have a way of never quite happening. Capitalism collapses when it is overthrown by revolution or when the conditions of relative economic freedom it requires for effective operation are denied by democratic governments in the name of social justice. There are no hidden laws or causes; just the wills of men. The present outlook for capitalism is not good in all truth—not because of some predetermined mechanism which will bring about its programmed demise, but because prevailing moral seriousness is weighted against it.

How can a new idealism for capitalist freedom and capitalist enterprise be conceived? There *is* a glimmer of light. For the very fickleness of intellectual opinion perhaps provides the opening required; and it is to a change in the attitudes of the leaders of educated opinion that we look for any hope of a remoralized appreciation of capitalism. The caricatures of the capitalist past, and the criticisms of capitalist society today, are so essentially emotional, rather than rational, in origin—despite what intellectuals themselves suppose about their commitments to ideals—that they are really very volatile. If their moral seriousness and their evident need to indulge their gifts for moral censoriousness can be redirected, capitalism can snatch a breathing space. I do not believe, as some do, that its survival will depend on its proven economic superiority—that when the present difficulties of inflation and recession are past, capitalism will lose some of its tarnish. The hostile critique of capitalism by social thinkers is too long-standing, and now too well-established, for that. Its survival, on the contrary, depends upon a shift of opinion within the élite who define the nature of public debate and set the dogmas of contemporary moralism in the minds of the young. There are surely already some indications, compared with the extravagancies of the later 1960s—when the intelligentsia were apparently beside themselves with their "crisis of values"—of a hardening of attitudes against too easy an acceptance of vapid social agonizing. So far there are only straws in the wind. The moment is a very critical one. It is up to the friends of capitalism to realise the solemnity of the task with which they are now confronted, and to appreciate the cost to human life if they fail. Capitalism has a good case to argue. It is the case of freedom.

On Black, White, Gray, and the Rainbow

Martin E. Marty

Dean E. R. Norman complains that intellectuals, and not least of all theological and ecclesiastical elitists in the West, have fallen into the habit of denigrating capitalism. With due apologies to those who see racial connotations in the choice of terms that white people often use, I point out that to denigrate is to "blacken" (*de* + *nigrare* = to blacken) the reputation of something or someone. His essay is an attempt simply to divide all ranks, an effort at providing two boxes of labels. Either you blacken capitalism or you whiten it. That's that.

Such an approach may alert the public to a need for better economic discriminations. But it also calls for a decision that most "common people" and many intellectuals and theologians do not want to make, do not feel called to make, and do not find impulses in Christian witness and theology that force them to make. Both capitalism and socialism admit of so many species that simply to choose between whole *isms* must lead one to overlook something. Both choices are time-bound. In the Christian perspective, they are late emergences. If either is to be identified with the purposes of God, as partisans of both tend to identify them, God must have been notoriously slow to act to redeem the people.

Both pure-form capitalism and socialism are being transformed. They are passing away, if they have not already passed away. To call the Christian world to a defense of the ephemeral may be humanistically noble. It can be morally satisfying to mourn the artifacts of this world. But to connect the passing with the eternal purposes of God is dangerous. I do not say that Canon Norman insists that God can work or has worked only through one economic system during the past several millennia, but his essay leaves us little choice but to reject in God's name one system of present-day economic argument and to adopt and defend the other.

Such an approach does not do justice to the shades of gray with which most people live, have to live, and want to live. Worse, it fails to foresee a rainbow of possibilities that might well be emergent from God's unfolding word and purpose, from human ingenuity, and from new practical circumstances.

I begin with such a statement of color preferences for personal reasons which need a moment's attention. A friend found the first draft of my response to Norman too indecisive. It seemed, he suggested, a covert if not overt defense of socialism. Could I make clear where I stood personally? Like Canon Norman he wanted to pose an economic-systems choice in the spirit of "he that is not with us is against us."

If it is helpful to readers, let me state that I do not remember ever having written anything in defense of communism or socialism, either under those names or in disguise, and I do not intend this response to be such a defense. I draw salary as a tenured professor from a modern private university whose resources have been amassed in part because of the generosity of people who have made their fortunes off early unfoldings of the capitalist system. That does not mean that I must be an endorser of all the means by which they gained their wealth. Many of these means were "mixed," from an ethical point of view. Some were almost criminally inhumane. I am free to criticize those who acquired wealth and their means, to protest against the perpetuation of these means, and to seek alternatives to them. But I have never thought it good faith to join with professors who call for revolutionary and radical action to overthrow the capitalist system, and then retire to the faculty club for drinks and conversations about the private schools to which they send their daughters.

Reasons for rejection of simple socialist systems for me, as for most people I know, run the range from trivial personal annoyances to philosophical convictions. I do not like to stand in line or fill out forms, and socialists do enlarge lines and lengthen forms. My philosophical differences run less to the issues of economic choice, about which I have concern but not professional competence to judge, than to moral, intellectual, and religious choice. When I outline these differences, Canon Norman might well feel that I am safely in the capitalist camp, vintage 1776.

The advocates of revolutionary socialism, whether they ground their advocacy in Christian millennialism, in mixed Christian and Marxian "liberation theology," or in simple secular philosophies of history, cannot point—or at least have not pointed to my satisfaction —to postrevolutionary resolutions that allow for true intellectual or religious freedom. They complain about "repressive tolerance" in our own current society without letting us point to the "repressive *in*tolerance" of socialist regimes elsewhere. They may say that I am demonstrating the provincialism of a Westerner with a full stomach when I cherish religious freedom without noting that other economic systems bring fuller stomachs. They have not shown that such systems are all that provident. And they slide past the murder of perhaps 7,000,000 under Maoism or of too many millions to count under the Stalinist system (which none of them any longer favors or even likes to hear brought up), and past the persecution that most postrevolutionary socialisms enact. To be told that such systems tolerate "religious freedom," because some of them allow churches to remain open so long as church people do not criticize the regime, is to leave us no further along than we would be under right-wing regimes in, say, Korea or Chile.

Life is lived not with the black and white of two stark alternatives but in the shades of gray of day-to-day choice and in the hope that a whole range of other alternatives might emerge. If Christianity to date has lived with six or eight economic systems, why can it not live with ten or twelve? To be told that it has prospered most under capitalism begs many historical questions. How does one define prosperity? Protestantism did advance into outposts around the world during capitalist expansion in the nineteenth century, but Christianity has often spread elsewhere without capitalist company. English and American entrepreneurs generously supported the churches during the rise of capitalism, but the church has found more lavish support under systems that one would find abhorrent. Some exemplary theology and piety and moral life have emerged under congenial forms of capitalism, but most Christian theology and piety did not. It does not take an Aleksandr Solzhenitsyn to remind us that congenial systems sap moral and spiritual courage and vision—which is why Solzhenitsyn is such a vigorous enemy of pluralist democracy and capitalist economies. In sum: in the eternal purposes of God no system, however attractive it be (and I find pluralistic democracy attractive), is integral to the fulfillment of divine purpose and none merits uncritical response.

It may be true, as Canon Norman and other defenders of "democratic capitalism" imply, that however many shades of gray or colors of the rainbow there may be, one finally must choose between systems that allow for greater initiative by individuals on the one hand or by collectives on the other. Given such a broad spectrum, my choice is closer to the individual side, but necessary qualifications of that preference will take the fun out of the commitment for those who insist on a simple choice between two competing systems.

Capitalism depends not only on elitist arguments and enterprisers' ingenuity. It relies also in part on circumstances. In order to be capitalist one must have something to be capitalist about. England, the United States, Western Europe, and other centers of capitalism after the 1770s possessed mineral resources, energy supplies, rich farmlands for production of raw materials, and the like. In many nations of the world there is little about which to be capitalist. One should not expect from these nations an emergence of something comparable to the Western polity.

Those of us who are depressed by the limited time allowed by "nonrenewable" energy resources and who have seen very little individualist or voluntary restraint in the use of them to date expect some increase in social control in the decades ahead. This may be the case until "renewable" resources are developed and while the public staggers under the inevitable inflation that must come with scarcity. Some of us fear authoritarian collectivism in an age of such shortages, or perhaps in an era when surveillance of terrorists becomes an attractive necessity, or when, for a variety of reasons not born of ideology, common people, not elites, "give up on the system."

Even those who claim to cherish individual intellectual freedoms foresee collectivist scenarios for such days. Thus Robert Heilbroner, though no religionist himself, expects that a coercive statist religion will emerge to hold a new system together. Heilbroner has noted that meanwhile "economic patriotism is on the decline, especially for believers in the orthodox capitalist faith," and that the building up of private morale has taken the place of support for "social morale."[1] On those grounds he ought to cheer E. R. Norman for making an effort, even though he will not agree with the defense.

Norman acts as if he is spitting into the wind, as if few are on the side of capitalism. In America his complaint has little grounding. The accounting, economics, and business majors outpace all others in colleges, and the masters of business administration symbolize the premium placed on capitalist professions by graduate students. But many of these are in the "I'll get mine" school of thought and have not reasoned about the system as Norman asks them to do.

---

[1] Robert Heilbroner, *Business Civilization in Decline* (New York: W. W. Norton, 1976), pp. 112, 115.

Let me compare my rejection of the tyranny of Norman's false alternatives to the kind of support and criticism that I give the nationalism of *my* nation. Through a career-long dedication to the study of American religious history I have found many reasons to applaud America, the colonies and the nation. My tastes are catholic: Bartolomé de Las Casas, John Winthrop, Abraham Lincoln, Reinhold Niebuhr, John Courtney Murray, Martin Luther King, and a hundred million simple worshippers are all in the gallery of heroes and heroines. I can almost stand with the Abraham Lincoln that critic Edmund Wilson described: Lincoln made "the union" a subject of religious mysticism.

Yet it was that same Abraham Lincoln who also fought against a simple defense of the nation. The Almighty has His own transcendent purposes. We should seek to follow His will, so far as it can be known, but we should not claim Him for our side—as liberation theologians and capitalist advocates of many sorts and schools tend to do.

Let us then applaud Norman for an attempt to move beyond support for private exploitation of the capitalist system and to the search for public morale in support of it. Applaud him for nettling un-self-critical elites in English religion or the World Council of Churches, as we are told he has done. Cheer him for pointing to some of the follies in their positions, for smoking out aspects of "the sociology of knowledge" that such elites would like to have us overlook. Praise him for making tentative steps toward the first outline of a new intellectual defense of capitalism as an alternative. But I temper my enthusiasm as I see the limits of applicability of his approach, at least in America.

His impression that he is blowing against the *Zeitgeist* is confusing if not deceiving. Neither the colleges, the service clubs, the business communities, the general public, nor the church-going citizenry in America include many who describe themselves as "liberal," to say nothing of "socialist" and to hint nothing of "communist." Norman and his kind are riding a tide. If we want to be accurate in assessment of contemporary power, we had better know so.

Then how account for the denigrators, the blackeners of capitalism that he does locate? To do justice to them one would have to treat them discretely and not as he does in the lump. One would have to discern the variety of their motives and not, as he does, to assign motives to them.

Noncapitalist or anticapitalist Christian language is understandable in nations that have never been capitalist and know no possibility of turning so now. Many representatives of churches in such nations are in the World Council of Churches or the Roman Catholic and Orthodox churches and councils. (Northern hemisphere theologians and ecclesiastics who simply accept their critiques in what Americans call a "yassuh" spirit of self-denigration may merit Norman's criticism.) We ought also to know that the "Third World" people are not necessarily transcending *their* circumstances in the name of the Christian word, any more than are "First World" leaders who defend their own systems. But there is no reason to see bad faith in their allegiances.

In the camp of the critics of capitalism there are also Westerners who through the centuries never did buy into it, including communitarians and millennialists who have also never said one appreciative word of secular socialism. Among these are Hutterites, Amish, Mennonites, and members of the Bruderhof, statistically minuscule groups who have had influence beyond their numbers. Also in this camp are many conservative and even biblicist evangelical groups and Catholic orders who may be naive about secular economics but who are exemplary in their search for alternatives to our two competing systems. They cannot be accused of bad faith for withholding allegiance to secular capitalism.

The transmitters of Norman's outlook in America have to be alert to apparent differences in our cultures. Thus he says that in English schools *"all"* the solutions of teachers "emphasize more collectivism." While the John Birch Society may make the same claim in America, anyone who has observed local school boards reviewing textbooks knows that textbook producers here have to be careful lest *any* of their solutions emphasize more collectivism. Again, it may be that in the tall towers of bureaucracy in Geneva and London, in New York or Washington, there may be some who feel that the World Council of Churches "may . . . prove to have been one of the forces making for the extinction of religion as well as freedom." But in the provinces, Christians either remember the Council's earlier and better contributions, make distinctions between good and bad Council activities, or do not know of or give a fig about the existence of the Council at all.

Norman's ad hominem arguments about numbers and motives of intellectual elites are not grounded in empirical analyses. If he has made them, he does not cite them. I know that some academic journals in the social sciences are a forum for Marxists in America, and I know that they generate a self-propagating but generally unheeded elite. But I have shared the platform with *"the* campus

29

Marxist" at many commencements and seen that he or she is seldom more than the titillater who reminds the masters of business administration that there is another and a forbidden world "out there." I know that in the Roman Catholic world some academic centers take rise from religious orders tied to the "Third World" in which Marxist-style liberation theology gets a hearing. But most Catholic seminarians of the last ten years, according to every survey I have seen, are conservative pietists and pastors who have little interest in the economic order or social action. Protestant-based and ecumenical theological schools have their leftish house-liberationist in some cases. They, too, titillate students and clienteles. But the students head for quiet pastorates, the clienteles are firm capitalists, and the liberationists can easily confer in the space of a phone booth. Those that I know approach their commitments from such a vast range of Christian and secular bases and personal experiences that the Norman stereotypes do a disservice to them.

Is there anything in the Norman *substance* to applaud? Yes. He smokes out progressivist and utopian metaphysics in some of the anticapitalist Christian expressions, as Paul Tillich also did in 1936 in *On the Boundary*. Tillich contended for the vision of a "consciousness of the 'corruption of existence,' a repudiation of every kind of social Utopia (including the metaphysics of progressivism), and an awareness of the irrational and demonic nature of existence" in Christianity.[2] So did Reinhold Niebuhr, who shared Norman's pessimistic view of human nature, but whom Norman would have found to be incorrigibly on the left. It is also good to be reminded of Original Sin and self-interest in all economic choices, though why Norman thinks capitalism should have a monopoly on that Christian doctrine is not made clear. Lutherans like to talk about humans being *simul justus et peccator*, at the same time justified and a sinner. Cannot Christians at large in their economic life also both be *simul* aware of their own self-interests and capable of rising above them? Societies are not likely to move toward altruism. I would be content to see long-range self-interest replace short-range self-interest in them. Because some elements in the capitalist orderings of existence have done so, I have some hope that they can be carried over and transformed in emergent orders.

I take it that the core "thing" for which Norman wants to generate morale in support of capitalism can be summarized in his lines: "Capitalism aspires to the realization of an enlightened self-

---

[2] Paul Tillich, *On the Boundary* (New York: Scribner's, 1936), p. 75.

interest; to educate men into a more rational social state, by the productive use of their selfish instincts. That is its moral purpose." Where capitalism has not lived up to that aspiration, it stands under judgment like all other systems. But is this sentence the best defense of capitalism, historically or ideologically?

That some capitalists *have* realized and *risen above* "enlightened self-interest" is historically demonstrable. I can confirm it in my personal experience; "some of my best friends are capitalists." They are often Christians whose understanding of faith and way of life outpace those of small leftish elites in the theological world. If we are to build "social morale" for the defense of elements of capitalism, it would be better to understand what makes them tick than to spend time misreading motives and overestimating the power of elites that denigrate capitalism.

Some sort of "mixed" pattern that draws on features of capitalism and socialism has begun to emerge and is likely to prevail. It is important to help such an order become humane and liberating. It is more urgent to do that than to call Christians to a "whitening" of the world of Adam Smith and the 1770s, for which I have some taste, the world of the Social Darwinists of the 1870s, for which I have none, or the world of the masters of business administration of the 1970s, who need much more help than Norman's essay and approach can give them.

Religion and the Demise
of Capitalism

James V. Schall

*To my great regret, I have to add the Christian Churches to the list of those
whose social outlook now contributes to the subversion of capitalism.*

E. R. Norman

Ever since the days of R. H. Tawney and Max Weber, when, for
cultural reasons, it seemed imperative to associate religion with
economic growth so that it would not be stigmatized as antimodern,
we have been aware of the subtle relationship between spiritual
movements and the growth of capitalism. E. R. Norman's perceptive
essay, welcome albeit perhaps too late, brings to the fore the opposite
perspective, that of religion's direct contribution to the potential
demise of capitalism.[1] Along with this, we have become increasingly
aware of the consequences to religion should it be eventually seen
to have been a major factor in the loss of world productive capacity
and civil freedom. Thus, if certain spiritual and theological doctrines
were in fact contributory to the preparation and development of
capitalism, we should not be overly surprised that capitalism will most
likely be undermined not by changes in material production but by
alterations of belief and ethical value.

Just as Max Weber suspected Marx wrong in his initial premises
about the priority of matter to spirit in social causation, so Father
Norman suspects the clerical and intellectual followers of Marx today
equally wrong in their analysis of the spiritual forces needed to make
and keep mankind human and prosperous. Norman's biting stricture
concerning the World Council of Churches could be applied to several
Catholic movements and intellectuals without changing a comma:

> The World Council of Churches, I need hardly say, is an
> international agency well-known for the partisan nature of
> its judgments and activities. It is an enemy of capitalism;

---

[1] In addition to the lecture printed above, see also Dr. Norman's *Christianity and
the World Order* (New York: Oxford University Press, 1979).

in the long term, it may even prove to have been one of the forces making for the extinction of religion as well as freedom.[2]

To this, I would add that the religious opposition to contemporary capitalism—which it makes little effort to distinguish from laissez faire capitalism—may also put it in the ranks of those extinguishing productivity, as well as freedom and religion.

These are, no doubt, stern charges. But it is now becoming evident that, as a result of the little noted demise of an identifiable and independent Catholic social thought as an alternative to laissez faire capitalism or socialism, the Marxists have co-opted wide segments of Catholic social thought and of the institutions designed to promote it. (In his address at Puebla, Mexico, John Paul II stoutly reaffirmed the independence of Catholic social thought, on January 28, 1979.) I believe the reason for this is not unrelated to some of the initial problems examined by Weber and Tawney, especially the question of the relationship of the Latin countries to the Protestant ones during the early successes of capitalism. Whatever the validity of the Protestant Ethic thesis or the reservations about it of von Brentano, George O'Brien, Amintore Fanfani, Werner Sombart, and others who attribute the nature of capitalism in Catholic areas to other social causes besides religion, the Latin South has always suffered something of an inferiority complex; it has itself suspected that its religion has been the principal cause of its backwardness.

At first sight, it would seem that the reaction to this criticism might have been to imitate the work ethic or the initiative system, and to adapt the technology, a path followed by Japan almost alone outside Europe. Inside Europe, on the other hand, with the exception of France the old Latin South was left behind along with its farflung colonies, areas in which the attack on capitalism today seems most vociferous. The riches garnered from the world in the sixteenth century by Spain and Portugal seemed to end up through the balance of trade in the prosperous North. As the eighteenth and nineteenth centuries went on, however, the center of sociological attention began to shift from the marvels of productivity to the consequences in the population, which were not all good by any means. The British

---

[2] Ibid. See also the author's "From Catholic 'Social Doctrine' to the 'Kingdom of God on Earth,'" *Communio*, Winter 1976; "America and Recent Catholic Social Thought," *Faith and Reason*, Spring 1977; "Horizons for Productivity," *The Priest*, February 1979. Cf. also Ernest Lefever, *Amsterdam to Nairobi: The World Council of Churches and the Third World* (Washington, D.C.: Ethics and Public Policy Center, Georgetown University, 1979).

taught a studious Karl Marx how the poor actually lived in this productive process.

Yet, in the nineteenth century it was still remembered that things had usually been much worse before the Industrial Revolution, so the intellectual analysis of poverty looked very different from the way it is seen today. Besides, the working classes, who attracted most of the sympathy of the analyzers, began to prosper. The case against capitalism was not all bad. In this context, Marxism itself became split over the analysis of how to account for this unexpected result. Capitalism, furthermore, began to be harnessed to certain normative values, legal processes, and rules. Thus, it even became fashionable as this process continued to deny that the resulting system was "capitalist" in the pejorative sense, for it certainly was not just like the original abuses.[3]

With the emergence of the Third World, however, after World War II, there reappeared a modernization of Lenin's old imperialist thesis, which had sought to redefine the "exploited" since the proletariat in the industrial countries were becoming so rich. The Western workers, Lenin taught with the help of an English economist, were really rich at the expense of Third World peasants. And, as it turned out, most of this new Third World was ruled by Western-educated but local elites who almost invariably looked on the situation through the glasses of their socialist professors at the Sorbonne or the London School of Economics.[4] Political independence was to be followed by economic independence in an interdependent world, the lack of which was assumed to explain the failure of these newer countries to develop more rapidly. When political independence did not produce what was expected, the blame shifted from colonialism to neo-colonialism. Ironically, in this context, the only countries that did seem to learn the secret of rapid growth were those that did not adopt the old socialist rhetoric. The ASEAN countries have achieved very high growth rates, even higher than those of Germany and Japan, long the leaders. As *The Economist* of London often pointed out over the years, the rate of real progress is almost in inverse ratio to the size of governmental institutions and their control over the economy. This failure to develop led to a further embracing of the absolutist theory

---

[3] See Jacques Maritain, *Reflections on America* (New York: Scribner's, 1958), chapter 19. See also A. A. Berle and Peter Drucker on the nature of the capitalist revolution.

[4] See Daniel Moynihan, "The United States in Opposition," *Commentary*, March 1975; P. T. Bauer, "Western Guilt and Third World Poverty," *Commentary*, January 1976; Norman Macrae, "America's Third Century," *The Economist*, October 25, 1975; Irving Kristol, *Two Cheers for Capitalism* (New York: Basic, 1978).

of development in which religion came to be regarded as a force to aid in social cohesion for modernization.[5]

It also became necessary, however, to explain why the poor were poor rather than to answer the more central questions of why everyone else was not and what outlooks, values, or ethics enable the poor to become richer. To explain the widespread poverty acknowledged by everyone, Third World leaders relied on their leftist education and on easily manipulated population theses. Combined with the new enthusiasm for politics shown by many Christians, the case seemed closed for the socialist option. The poor were poor, it was blindly believed, because somebody "exploited" them. And with this marvelously useful, if terribly inaccurate, explanation, all of the old complexes of the Latin South and the socialist left rose again in a new form. Not only was the poorer part of the world in no sense responsible for its own fate, but there was a devil to blame for the general blight and plight. That devil was capitalism, with its economic instruments of profit and the corporation.

Consequently, the often-noted affinity of predominately Catholic countries for Marxist explanations served to divert attention from the harder issues of work, savings, education, innovations, and political stability, the real causes of prosperity. Moreover, if the poor are poor because they are "exploited," then the only real solutions are political action, down-with-the-oppressor movements, and revolution. As a result, the very ideas and institutions that might help alleviate poverty are themselves rejected or destroyed. Religion then seems to promote political action to establish an out-of-date, highly dangerous system, in which freedom is sacrificed for control of the economy and of civic expression. The old fear that religion is merely an adjunct of absolute power is apparently verified.

For such reasons, then, it can well be argued that the most important spiritual crisis facing Christianity today—and the culture that grew out of it—does revolve about the issue Father Norman raises, the relationship between religion and the economy. This is not the old issue, now something of a red herring, of indifference to the poor. No one, least of all the capitalists, is arguing for a Herbert Spencer type of survival of the fittest. Everyone involved, from socialists to capitalists, is attuned to the poor. The real debate is over what does in fact help them. What is neglected is attention to freely expressed personal and individual values as causes of development. The theory that is now dominant accepts without qualification the idea

---

[5] See David Apter, *The Politics of Modernization* (Chicago: University of Chicago Press, 1965).

that no one can be free unless he is fed, well-fed. Rousseau's notion of forcing people to be free has taken on a new twist.

It is no accident that the socialist-distributist ethos of the current intellectual atmosphere ignores the emphasis on personal choice and reward as the key motivation in an authentic humanist capitalism, however it be designated. Norman's emphasis is correct:

> For the morality of capitalism has first to do with the morality of choice; with the individual's freedom to select, either as producer or consumer, from among alternative sources of economic enterprise. It is the freedom left to the individual to have control over his own labour. . . . The competitive deployment of personal resources and talents is a tremendous stimulus to moral self-consciousness; it encourages, rather than discourages, the individual in the cultivation of a practical scheme of responsibility for his actions, and imposes, as a condition of maintaining living standards, a sense of moral duty.

This approach emphasizes, in a way no other system really does, the classic Christian idea of free choice as the personal locus of action, not merely inside oneself but also as it relates to others. Freedom is not something society gives to individuals but the converse, something that first must be given to those ultimate metaphysical realities that bear "society," the human persons that compose it.

Allied to the Christian-socialist type of shift to exploitation and statist theory is the reintroduction into contemporary thought, ironically often from religious sources, of one of the most dangerous ideas in all the history of thought, that of collective guilt. Under the easy rubric of "social sin," we see reestablished the idea that abstractions, separated relations, are responsible for evil in the world, that the good is the result of social organization and not primarily of personal choice. Acceptance of this idea is, it strikes me, one of the key causes for the "license to kill" that we see in the contemporary world, wherein members of corporations, countries, religions, and classes are eliminated not because of anything they personally may have done but because they "represent" the corporate system held to be somehow guilty. This sort of analysis, of course, follows from that side of modern political theory which, after Rousseau, looked for the causes of social evil not in individual choices but in property or political arrangements. Without denying that social systems do to some extent condition human choice, that some are better than others (as classic thought held about forms of government), still the concept of "social sin" as applied to capitalist practice is mainly the result of a hidden ideology that conceives human liberty only as an end-product of a controlled social system.

Undoubtedly, E. R. Norman is correct in noting the connection between a false optimism about what is to be expected from human nature and the practical denial of the Christian doctrine of Original Sin. Nothing marks the anticapitalist religious argument of recent times more than its naive confidence that the existing socialisms of our times have virtues not revealed by any cold analysis. The refusal to place actual results over hoped-for ideals is the classic mark of the ideologue. The degree to which religion has become mere ideology is nowhere more marked than here. The doctrine of Original Sin, on the contrary, led us to be cautious about all worldly enterprises, including the capitalist ones. It recognized that personal choice is always a drama involving the external order in its manifestations, and that this drama is in full vigor in every type of social order, the worst as well as the best. This meant, further, that any effort to relocate responsibility for human action outside the personal will reduced the value of the individual to that of a mechanism capable of manipulation by social policy.

The argument for "capitalism," on the other hand, is not intended to suggest that the performance of such a system is always best or wise. It can make serious mistakes and still be the best system available if rationally ordered. The theory of capitalism allows for its errors and mistakes. Yet, in the debate over this issue, Christopher Dawson's remark of 1951 is still pertinent:

> There is in fact a dualism between the marxist myth, which is ethical and apocalyptic, and the marxist interpretation of history, which is materialist, determinist, and ethically relativistic. But it is from the first of these two elements that communism has derived and still derives its popular appeal and its quasi-religious character which render it such a serious rival to Christianity.[6]

In other words, any defense of a democratic capitalism must confront the ethical, apocalyptic appeal in Marxism, which has held an enormous attraction for Christians. Latin theologians and politicians, especially, have turned to Marxism as a solution to the vast problems of world order. The real issue for them is not what really alleviates poverty, but rather what fulfills the ultimate needs of mankind. The disadvantage of Father Norman's approach is that its sane practicality

---

[6] Christopher Dawson, "The Christian Vision of History," in *The Dynamics of World Order*, ed. J. J. Mulloy (New York: Mentor, 1956), p. 245.

does not stress the metaphysics that must satisfy the deeper needs of man. Christians, when they fail to realize the limits or ultimate values of their faith, seem peculiarly susceptible to this-worldly perfectionist movements.

Capitalism may still solve many of our worldly problems, but it will not answer the deeper theological and spiritual needs of mankind. E. R. Norman has suggested that the central values of the Western Christian tradition may be imperative to any free and productive approach to the problems of the poor, if the primacy of freedom and the possibility of religion are to be retained, and if something concrete is to be done about the poor. It is becoming clear, however, that those most attracted to a Marxist solution are not the poor but rather the clerical and intellectual classes who have lost living contact with Christian metaphysical approaches, and whose guilt, as E. R. Norman suggests, limits their practicality.

In practice, then, the denial of capitalism has roots in the meaning of religion, especially in the kind of ultimate happiness it proposes to man. St. Augustine is still vital to an understanding that the City of God is not to be identified with an Earthly City. We should not be surprised that Christians are tempted by a this-worldly absolutism, for that possibility is the essence of freedom and its misuse. Most Christians are better prepared to understand the power of an ethical and apocalyptic movement than the secularist who has no understanding of absolute good or order. Professor Norman has re-emphasized that freedom is the basis of any truly human order, system, or well-being. We must ask Christians who are tempted by the Marxist solutions whether they are still members of that faith that once gave rise to capitalism. The demise of capitalism, in the end, may be more perplexing than its rise. In any case, undoubtedly, both capitalism and Marxism possess religious, Christian origins.

Truly Human Dreams

Bernard Cooke

However one might wish to disagree with Dr. Norman on some of his judgments, he is certainly correct in saying that there has been very little serious theological justification of capitalism in recent years. He is correct, too, in suggesting that some writing and speaking on economic/political matters has been a sloganish and shrill advocacy of socialism as a solution to "the evils caused by capitalistic imperialism." On the other hand there is a considerable body of analysis ranging from Peter Berger to Wallace Clement to Pope Paul VI to Denis Goulet that can help define the pertinent issues and put them into perspective. All this suggests to me the need for cool-headed, though morally committed, discourse among groups of people who could together study the "ethics of capitalism." Such discourse would have to be a continuing affair, involving persons with real expertise in a number of relevant fields, aimed at genuine discovery and not legitimation, and dealing not just with theoretical principles but with practical judgments about the real world of present-day economic life. Ultimately the final *moral* judgment about economic activity must be made by those involved in this activity (which, of course, in one way involves all of us), for it is only the practical prudential decision that can be the concrete moral judgment.

Attempts such as our present exercise of exchanging views in a collection of essays can be a step in this direction, but I must confess to uneasiness regarding the extent to which the charged atmosphere of the "capitalism versus socialism" discussion works against an objective reading of these essays. Discussion about the respective "morality" of capitalism and socialism has consistently been plagued by the penchant for generalizations on the part of proponents for one or the other position, and it would only increase the fogginess if

I were to add some *theological* generalities. Perhaps most basically, I am not clear what precisely are the parameters of our debate—and I say that not to be negative but to suggest that there is a great need to clarify the very terms of the argument before we can hope to come to intelligent agreement or disagreement.

When, for example, should one talk about a given context as an instance of capitalism? To take my own geographical situation: I live in a province of Canada, which does have some features that might be classified as socialist, such as the publicly owned telephone and transportation systems (including a province-owned airline) and a rather comprehensive health-care program; yet, it would be hard to imagine a provincial government more totally committed to the interests of large-scale business enterprises. Or again, in trying to appraise the human aspects of capitalism, is one talking about the effects of industrializing productivity, or about the distribution of wealth, or about technology's potential for depersonalizing human existence, or what? In any of these, is one dealing with the intrinsic and necessary functioning of a given system or is one dealing with injustices that come from abuse of the system? Given these ambiguities, I propose—unfortunately in all too general fashion—six challenges that religion, and specifically, Christianity, makes to any economic system. If my remarks end up sounding too exclusively and critically directed at capitalism, that is only because capitalism is the topic under discussion. Frankly, I do not believe that Christianity is meant to be wedded to any particular political, economic, or social theory or pattern; I believe that no given system is the best possible for humans, the one most compatible with Christianity's vision and hopes. I do, however, think it possible that a given system be at the moment more in accord with that vision or, on the contrary, be radically opposed to the realization of that vision or hope. Therefore, this is the question Christian theology should address: Does capitalism (or any other economic system) allow humans to realize the condition of life that Christianity defines as their birthright, or is it intrinsic to capitalism that some humans be deprived of this destiny? Theology by itself cannot respond to this question; what it can do is describe, from a religious perspective, the condition of life that would be appropriately human.

1. First, then, as a Christian theologian I wish to see how capitalism contributes to the acquisition by all persons of that freedom and equality that is their due and, on the basis of such freedom and equality, how capitalism fosters the community essential to what Christians call "the establishment of the kingdom of God." Chris-

tianity is not simplistic in its understanding either of freedom or of equality. It is quite cognizant of what Paul in his letters calls "a diversity of gifts" and of differing motivations, efforts, and contributions to human well-being. As a result Christianity recognizes that justice itself demands differences in social or economic rewards and in social, economic, and political position; but from its origins, Christianity has maintained that Jesus of Nazareth came to break down barriers between humans as persons. In Galatians, the first socially dividing distinction declared to be incompatible with Christianity is ethnic—"neither Jew nor Greek"; but the second is economic/social— "neither slave nor free." If the economic aspect of this negated distinction is not clear enough in Galatians, it is unmistakable in the Gospel parable of Dives and Lazarus.

Responsible studies indicate that the progressive well-being of a capitalistic economy is linked with the continuing poverty of a certain portion of the human race. This is not just a matter of being less affluent: it is a question of building poverty and unemployment into economic planning, a question of denying indigenous development (whether industrial or agricultural) to certain regions of the world so that they remain sources of raw material for industrial production elsewhere, a question of increasing numbers of humans finding themselves reduced to economic powerlessness as the real power of economic decision passes into ever fewer hands. Barbara Ward's writings, beginning with her *Rich Nations and the Poor Nations*, Wallace Clement's *Canadian Corporate Elite* and *Continental Corporate Power*, and Richard Barnet and Ronald Mueller's *Global Reach* raise the unavoidable question of capitalism's relation to a systemic deprivation of freedom, dignity, and opportunity for a large portion of humanity. These analyses cannot be easily dismissed. A theological look at capitalism must ask whether these radical social and economic inequalities are intrinsically tied to industrial capitalism or whether, on the other hand, under capitalism all men and women can have sufficient economic well-being and self-determination to achieve dignity and equality and to develop their human potential.

2. A second area of theological analysis of socio-economic structures that poses questions to capitalism (or to any other system) is the role of profit as a motivation, criterion of operation, and measure of success. If I do not misread the classical moral outlook of the world's great religions, the responsibility of any individual or institution (such as a multinational corporation) in a society to foster the common good of that society takes precedence over the right to seek more narrow advantage, such as financial gain or increase of

personal or corporate power. This outlook does not rule out either economic gain or social power as inappropriate goals of human behavior; it says only that bounds should be set on the quest for such goals and that "the common good" is normative in the determination of these bounds. Individuals and groups have a right to benefit from the productivity of an industrialized capitalist system, but the extent of this benefit must be governed by their obligation in justice to contribute to the overall good of the human condition. Certainly industrial and business enterprises must plan for enough return on investment to remain healthy, but the principle should be maintained: such enterprises have a responsibility to contribute to the good of society. That is a more normative discipline than the discipline of profit, to which Norman quite rightly refers.

One does not know how seriously to take the remark, "We're in business for only one reason, to make a profit," but it is practically an axiom in some discussion about ethics of the business world. The statement is a truism if it means, "No business can prosper or even survive if it loses money. And besides, we obviously deserve a reasonable profit for our efforts, creative ideas, and risk." But if the statement means that profit is the sole purpose or even the ultimate purpose of industrial or commercial activity, a basic cleavage in values between religion and business appears. And one who espouses the traditional values of Judaism and Christianity, based on the superiority of persons over things, must take exception. I cannot see why a fundamental and controlling intention to contribute to the genuine welfare of all members of society would work against the healthy development of business and industry, nor why it would not allow an appropriate measure of reward for all those involved in industrial production, distribution, marketing, and financing. But perhaps something intrinsic in capitalism as a financial system requires that profit, even accelerating profit, determine policy. If this is so, persons end up being subordinate to things.

3. Dr. Norman recognizes quite clearly that a realistic approach to human economic behavior must take account of human greed, and he does so in a category familiar to biblical thought and Christian theology: Original Sin. This is the notion that sin is inherent in human nature, is not rooted in any system, such as capitalism, and is inherited by each human at birth. There is a common tendency to interpret this concept as a basic inclination of humans toward evil. Even if one wishes to give a more careful exegesis of the revelant biblical passages and a more sophisticated theological explanation of the reality involved, human greed, exploitation, and violence seem to

confirm the notion that something is basically wrong. Practically, this means that religion must preach conversion and society must govern people's behavior.

When one applies this notion to a capitalistic society, one comes face to face with the basic problem of greed: greed for wealth and greed for power—and not just on the part of capitalists. The question of "systemic evil," the way in which systems and structures can embody forces destructive of human individuality, appears increasingly in any discussion of Original Sin. Theoretically, of course, it is always possible for those in decision-making positions in a capitalistic system to formulate their policies to honor social justice. Given, however, the presence of Original Sin in all humans and the additional temptation provided to the rich and powerful, can we realistically expect the decision makers to be self-governing? History, without question, gives us cause to respond negatively.

Advocates of capitalism must do one of two things: either prove that those at the focus of power are free from Original Sin or suggest methods of social-political governance that effectively confine the activities of industrial capitalism to the dictates of justice. Norman, as I read him, does neither: he accepts the universality of Original Sin, and he trusts the dialectic of enlightened self-interest to provide the necessary brake on evil behavior. Although somewhat optimistic about a future in which corporations and governments will work together in controlled harmony, Neil Jacoby's *Corporate Power and Social Responsibility* strikes me as more realistic in accepting the need for some governance from outside the capitalist enterprise itself. The good that capitalism promises to provide will benefit all humans only if the temptations intrinsic to the system are controlled. The question is, Is this possible?

4. The fourth question Christian theology poses to capitalism is the question of just price. Justice suggests that a capitalistic economy should operate to provide for people's real needs—nourishment, housing, communication, and the like. Yet, one could argue that in today's world, people's genuine needs are exploited and artificial needs created to feed the growth of economic processes. Instead of people's needs acting as a brake on prices, the costs of such basics as food and housing rise as need becomes greater. The law of pricing seems to be "whatever the market will bear": How far can consumers be pushed until they find it absolutely impossible to buy? Even if some consumers are driven out of the market (presumably into relative starvation or homelessness), higher prices allow the same or even greater profit on smaller volume.

Responses such as "people never had it so good" are irrelevant, even if they were true. The basic question is justice—the things to which people have a right if they are participating agents in a productive society, the balance between possession by all people of freedom of opportunity based in secure and comfortable human living and the possession by a few of unnecessary wealth and economic power. Some governing of the pricing structures in the economy is necessary; and if there is any truth in the often-voiced contention that any form of outside control will disrupt the capitalist economy, the Christian theologian should doubt the acceptability of capitalism. There is, then, a pressing need to develop within capitalist principles a system of just pricing that affords all people a decent standard of living.

5. Whether one agrees or disagrees with him, Karl Marx clearly put his finger on a basic issue when he questioned the nature and function of work in a capitalistic society. This is an issue Christian theology cannot ignore. To adapt another biblical saying, work is for the sake of humans, not humans for the sake of work. The Bible recognizes that work is often tedious and burdensome but sees this to be the result of sin, that is, not the way things ought to be: the role of humans in the world should be creative.

One should not place too heavy a burden, however, on the few scriptural passages that deal directly with work; what is more important is the Bible's evolving insight into the primacy of the person. There is an ultimacy about a man or a woman, and consequently about human activity, that resists total subordination to processes. Work obviously fits into the productive processes of any human society, including the processes of industrial capitalism; but this very work is also the expression of human consciousness and intention— at least if it is to be called human. Because of its role in human experience—a role so basic we use it as a distinguishing human characteristic in the term "homo faber"—work cannot be considered simply a commodity to be bought and sold as a transaction of economic life.

Compensation should be given for work, but this means more than basic economic compensation, which must be determined in accord with distributive justice. The intrinsic compensations of achievement, self-expression, fulfillment of responsibility, and creativeness (proportionate to the kind of work involved) must also be present or work becomes not only dehumanized but dehumanizing. No sector of society has the right to dehumanize laborers, especially when the laborers have no alternative means of survival. To buy labor without consideration of its human impact is akin to buying the persons involved; it can easily become a form of slavery.

The theologian can point out the value of the person and of human activity that must be respected in work; whether capitalism can honor this value must be answered by social scientists. Certainly, the evidence of actual practice during the past few centuries indicates that this is a very real question. We need to listen today not just to statistics and analyses but to the voices of those such as David Sheppard in his *Built as a City* who with Christian sympathies and mature and educated understanding of the modern world have shared the everyday life of the laboring people.

6. One of the most frequently misused passages in the Bible is the passage in Genesis that speaks of God giving to humans dominion over the earth. A misreading of this text has been appealed to time and time again to justify human exploitation of the earth and its resources. Adam is described in Genesis as a gardener who can enjoy the fruits of the soil, but human sovereignty refers primarily to the human transmission of life. Though there are clear overtones of human responsibility for the present world, the deeper biblical principle implies the right of future generations to live in a world that allows for their happiness and achievement, a world that has not been stripped of its fruitfulness and beauty.

Here we touch upon the present outlook and marketing practice of capitalistic economies, namely the emphasis on usage rather than care of natural resources. Again we must ask whether this is intrinsic or accidental to capitalism as an economic system. Unquestionably, it is hard to balance employment opportunity and environmental conservation; but the large-scale production of unnecessary items for the affluent at the price of diminishing irreplaceable resources (such as petroleum) makes one think that the profit motive has overruled ethical considerations.

It is all too easy for industry and business to justify such production by claiming that they provide only what people desire. First, however, the reference to "people" as potential buyers excludes the majority of humans who obviously have no means of buying extravagant items. Second, there is a conscious and assiduous fostering of such desires through expensive and highly skilled advertising, whereas the socially responsible industrial and commercial agencies should encourage restraint and care. Third, the advertised "conversion" of big corporations to environmental concerns becomes suspect when one observes their constant resistance to restrictions on pollution of air, water, and land. One also wonders if our present agencies for governing such exploitation are sufficient to avoid catastrophe.

Such advertising and marketing raises people's expectations and results in social discord and division. The discrepancy between "have" and "have not" groups in society is a basic injustice that becomes a potentially explosive social situation when the "have nots" perceive the discrepancy, as is true today. If social upheaval and war mark the next few decades, the unfulfilled expectations of the earth's disadvantaged people will be a major cause. The unending appeal to "buy what you don't yet have" corrodes the values even of the affluent. From an ethical and theological perspective one cannot help but question the marketing techniques governed only by the norm of increased sales. Capitalistic enterprises are not meant to perform religion's role of conversion to a more idealistic view of life. But as responsible agents in society they bear part of the burden of fostering genuinely human outlooks and ways of life.

In the final analysis the justification of industrial capitalism will be practical rather than theoretical. Like any other structuring of human life, it will prove or disprove itself by what it accomplishes. But what will act as the criterion in evaluating its performance? Christian theology can enter here into the arena of decision by proposing its view of what "human" means and its ideal of what is truly good for humans, both individually and socially.

One last remark: I still have the uneasy feeling that our discussion is out of date, that the economic/political/social structure of humanity has changed for the real questions to be treated in a capitalism versus socialism context. There are new systemic possibilities for good and evil that are not proper to either capitalism or socialism. As books like Galbraith's *New Industrial State* or Peter Drucker's *Age of Discontinuity* suggest, radical changes in procedures and structure are in progress, and these need to be analyzed and evaluated in themselves without being categorized as capitalist or socialist. And cultural options about such things as life style (which obviously intertwine with economics) may have very much to do with securing freedom and justice and peace. Perhaps in this fluid situation, theology's main function is to help people dream the truly human dreams and see truly human visions of the future.

Moving the Argument Forward

David B. Burrell

E. R. Norman's perceptive observations concerning the "denigration of capitalism" deserve attention for their specific merits, as well as offering us a way of measuring a growing body of critical commentary. That literature distinguishes itself precisely by questioning the norms of the prevailing social and political commentary. The commentators who prevail have rewarded the impious with a label designed to put them in their place: "the new conservatives." Coupled with convenient innuendo about the salaried allegiance of these new critics, the label should discredit them enough to avoid having to attend to their arguments.

A recurring ploy, such labeling hardly credits those who have championed freedom of inquiry, yet it does confirm those who see interest shaping intellectual endeavors overall. The ploy would probably work better than it has, however, were it not for the way the old critics have arrived. It is not simply the fact that they have arrived that should give us pause (as the label "new class" clearly makes us do), but also the *way* they have arrived: by invoking and inserting themselves into the machinery of government. Recourse of "liberals" to state protection was bound to stimulate a compensating resurgence of proponents of freedom. If our imaginations once linked "liberals" with freedom and "conservatives" with structure, we need only remind ourselves that labels are not descriptions, and that a reliable brand can lose its savor through corporate shuffling.

I.

So *freedom* emerges once again to question our social justifications and challenge our lived complicities. With freedom comes the individual, and with the individual a distrust of schemes and of ideologies.

So the defense of capitalism structures itself as a series of reminders about the centrality of choice: "The morality of capitalism has first to do with the morality of choice; with the individual's freedom to select." This style of economic organization presents itself as cultivating "the freedom left to the individual to have a control over his own labour." An inevitable social byproduct of so deliberate and systemic a support of freedom is to encourage "the individual in the cultivation of a practical scheme of responsibility for his actions," and hence of "a sense of moral duty."

Here we have the heart of Dean Norman's defense, which he chooses to pit directly against "the Marxist assertion that a man alienates his freedom and his personality by selling his labour to another." Norman employs the standard device for attenuating Marx's wholesale alienation critique, by proposing that "the conditions of work [be] adequately safeguarded, on both sides equally, at law." Papal encyclicals expand "conditions of work" to include commensurate participation in elaborating the goals and shaping the administration of an enterprise, yet the intent is the same: to alter enough key features in the work situation to deflect the critical purchase of the notion of alienation.

In fact, of course, this strategy has worked. The general amelioration of working conditions in the West has made it difficult for Marxism to take hold here. But it will not do as a defense of capitalism merely to present it as enhancing the scope of individual liberty. For there is much more to the system than that, and furthermore, we cannot make face-value declarations about economic choice after Marx, any more than we can make straightforward assertions about personal responsibility after Freud.

For just as each of these writers has spawned an ideology that can easily obscure, each has also posed a systemic criticism of social, economic, and individual life that cannot but enlighten those who grapple with it. Theoretical proposals as far-reaching as theirs need not be true to be illuminating. I shall argue that the strength of Norman's observations (and of others related to his) lies in their quality of observation. Such moves are critical in any arena where stereotype and ideology have come to prevail. Wittgenstein confronted a prevailing philosophical hegemony with the acerbic directive: Away from explanation; back to description! Clear observations of actual interactions will, moreover, be indispensable to any forthcoming defense of a system as protean as capitalism. Yet a degree of philosophical penetration at least as powerful as that of Marx must surely accompany anything so ambitious as a defense of capitalism.

I suspect, in fact, that some sustained study of Marx's writings would give the new critics more critical distance on their own efforts and release them from a narrowly defensive conception of their task. But I shall argue the case on more neutral philosophical grounds. Without questioning that "capitalism has a good case to argue," I shall question whether it can be described as "the case of freedom." The issue lies one step behind freedom—in agency and accountability —traditionally regarded as conditions of freedom. I shall propose that capitalism's case would be a good deal stronger than it is were its proponents to delineate how capitalism's very growth has severely altered these features, and how its success depends on creating within the new conditions a way of protecting the humanity and freedom of its agents.

II.

This proposal should make clearer sense of my references to Freud and to Marx. I am not recommending either view of the individual or of society. In fact, I would finally have to judge their overall analyses of the source and goal of human initiative to be false. Yet making that assessment—in both cases—forces one to grapple with a genuinely systemic analysis of human action. As a result we can only be the richer for confronting their thought. To grasp the dynamics latent in the key notions of transference (Freud) or alienation (Marx) is to feel the force of their analysis and to appreciate why Tawney regarded Marx as the last of the medieval scholastic thinkers. Marx did not hesitate to offer a theory purporting to explain the workings of the whole of human society.

A system that offers so much, of course, has its own seductiveness. Anglo-Saxons are less inclined to trust so comprehensive an explanation. Hence Norman can say, not without wisdom, that "one of the most advantageous features of capitalism [is] that it is *not* a systematic and rationalized ideology or structure." Rather than discourse on the common good, it "aspires to the realisation of an enlightened self-interest; . . . it accepts men as they are, and turns their instincts to the beneficial practices of personal and productive industry." The result, inevitably, is "a lot of loose ends, and the obloquy of the rationalist-minded theorists." Yet for all that, one can discern a "moral purpose" here: "to educate men into a more rational social state, by the productive use of their selfish instincts." And a realistic one as well.

Why, then, has capitalism such a bad press? Why has the system become nearly synonymous with exploitation? Why has socialism the ethical advantage, especially when its record is so spotty? Norman offers one plausible reason: the prevailing conviction "that capitalism may arguably have some practical advantages, but that it has no theoretical justification." If it cannot account for its superiority by showing how it reflects and contributes to a view of the human person that at once respects our limitations yet also resonates with our aspirations, then its success could well represent a fortuitous conjunction of historical accidents: a group of restless achievers, religiously motivated, suddenly found a continent to exploit. Furthermore, a singular political development had imbued them with a set of institutions that at once respected individual rights and maximized personal opportunity.

That group in this place could not help but be successful. But watch them wield the power of their success; note how they treat others as the religious base for mutual respect proved too narrow or even eroded away. How can other nations—lacking that peculiar mix of social, political, and economic factors—picture themselves adopting anything similar? What, moreover, can others make of us as they see us operating—for us, abroad; for them, in their own countries? It is here, I am convinced, where acknowledged absence of theoretical reflection becomes a baleful want of self-knowledge. When the American or European-based corporation meets the "other world," it not only suffers from a disastrous "press," but cannot even comprehend why. No matter how essential their dealings may be to the development of the countries in question, no one can overlook the accompanying load of resentment. Must this simply be borne, or can we learn something thereby about ourselves—something that we could put to use at home as well?

III.

It is these power discrepancies, I fear, that make capitalism's claim of "preserving freedom" ring hollow to so many. Thus the system suffers from its very success. But that observation cannot remain a simple fatalistic comment. We must find tools of analysis precise enough to lay bare how that accumulated power has substantially altered the conditions for acting and for accountability that give freedom its peculiar body.

Norman's strongest case for the moral purpose of capitalism turned on "the relationship between enterprise and personal moral character." Without prejudice to background conditions of fairness, one cannot help but acknowledge how "the competitive deployment of personal resources and talents is a tremendous stimulus to moral self-consciousness"—especially when contrasted to a hand-out syndrome. In Norman's felicitous phrasing, a society so organized "encourages, rather than discourages, the individual in the cultivation of a practical scheme of responsibility for his actions, and imposes, as a condition of maintaining living standards, a sense of moral duty."

I contend that the primary political, social, and economic actor in the dominant capitalistic world—the corporation—has, in the course of accumulating power, overlooked and failed to cultivate precisely those features of responsibility that have so distinguished the social, political, and economic fabric we call "free enterprise." This failure is especially evident when the Western corporation is acting in a foreign country relatively free of the "legislative restraint and charitable palliatives" that Norman acknowledges "the minor evils of capitalist society clearly need."

But it can also be observed at home when one corporation absorbs another, utilizes its "cash flow" to finance an entirely unrelated industry, then declares the purchased corporation "unprofitable," and so undermines the livelihood of an entire community. The more absent the ownership, the more readily can it invoke efficiency and profit without reference to other operating values. The result, as in Youngstown, is a living replica of the caricature Norman deplores, with real consequences in thousands of lives. Must a justification of capitalism justify maneuvers like these? And given the propensity towards corporate merger and transnational activity, can we any longer consider such maneuvers "minor evils"?

The answer must be no to both questions out of respect for the very sense of moral duty that Norman has shown democratic capitalism[1] imposes as a condition for its continued operation. That moral sense is grounded not in a code but in something far more basic: in a working scheme of responsibility for one's actions. Hence my concern for the twin conditions of freedom: agency and accountability. If the corporation assumes the role of a person under the law, that is precisely so it can properly be said to *act* in society.

---

[1] The expression "democratic capitalism" is not Norman's but Michael Novak's. He develops the three dimensions that history has woven together: social, political, and economic, and so names the result, in *The American Vision: An Essay on The Future of Democratic Capitalism* (Washington, D.C.: American Enterprise Institute, 1978). I find the metaphor of the "war of ideas" used throughout this work to be a perilously unprofitable one, in that it leads away from self-knowledge and an ideal of consistency with one's own ideals to an all too spontaneous preoccupation with "the enemy."

Yet agency and responsibility go hand in glove. If a corporation is to be an actor—and in a highly developed capitalist system, corporations are the actors par excellence—it cannot eschew normal human responsibilities. Moreover, if a corporation acts only by virtue of a felicitous legal fiction, the primary actors remain individuals. It follows that structuring corporations so that relevant individuals can evade their share of responsibility for the corporation's actions undermines the credibility and the utility of that original legal fiction. What is more, continuing structures that promote such evasive practices can only undermine the system that promised to enhance human freedom.

Yet well-known procedures for evading responsibility seem endemic to the bureaucratic management required to handle large-scale operations—whether they be organized for profit or not. And the minimalist sense in which a corporation can be an actor—it need not embody compassion, for example—can license it to behave like a monster when it is bereft of the normal constraints surrounding an individual when he or she acts. Hence the documented excesses attributed to absentee ownership in Appalachia and elsewhere.

The pressure for legal remedies in these cases reflects the inherent connection between agency and accountability. When I can get away without being recognized, it is almost as though I need not own up to the deed myself. Certainly Matthew 25, the scenario of a final reckoning, has had a powerful effect on Christians' sense of personal responsibility for their actions or omissions. Legal constraints are necessary but cannot substitute for a corporation's explicitly assuming responsibility for the effects of its actions on society, present and future.

Corporations must voluntarily assume responsibility—recognize the role they play and their consequent accountability to society—if one is to develop Norman's attempt at a theoretical justification of capitalism. It is demanded if the system is to be consistent with what it claims to contribute to humankind. What is more, there seems to be a strict parallel between the dilemmas in which individuals feel themselves caught as they attempt to function ethically within a corporate structure and those that chief executives and board members experience as they ponder the relations a corporation ought to recognize and pursue within society.[2]

---

[2] I am indebted to Kenneth Goodpaster for recognizing this isomorphism between the dilemmas faced by an individual manager and those that the corporation itself must contend with. See his "Morality and Organizations" in *Proceedings of Second National Conference on Business Ethics*, Bentley College, 1979. Re-

How must corporations be structured and perceived so they can assume responsibility for what they are doing? And how can this be accomplished in the face of an endemic tendency—bureaucratic and individual—to evade such responsibility?[3] This is the task facing capitalism if it would justify itself. Although it takes some careful analysis to understand the issues involved, the task itself is less theoretical than practical, so it should play into one of the strengths of this system. Or has the system met its peculiar demon here— self-interest so large and powerful that it can overlook the need to become enlightened? That is the question the situation today— domestic and international, social, political, and economic—raises in response to Dean Norman's perceptive essay.[4]

printed in T. Donaldson and P. Werhane, *Business Ethics* (Englewood Cliffs, N.J.: Prentice-Hall, 1979). Also his Introduction to *Policies and Persons: Dilemmas in Corporate Decision-Making* (Notre Dame, Ind.: University of Notre Dame Press, 1979).

[3] Herbert Fingarette has carefully located the roots of self-deception in a systemic failure to "spell out" one's engagements, in *Self-Deception* (New York: Humanities Press, 1969). Each of us can understand his analysis all too well; a study of the ways in which corporate structures and policies embody a corresponding disingenuousness could be similarly sobering.

[4] Charles W. Powers has tried to meet this sort of question realistically in Yale Brozen, Elmer Johnson, and Charles Powers, *Can the Market Sustain an Ethic?* (Chicago: University of Chicago Press, 1978).

New Questions for Humanists

Michael Novak

The literature about the "denigration of capitalism" is already extensive. In 1954, Friedrich A. Hayek edited a series of substantial essays, including one on American intellectual history by Louis Hacker, in *Capitalism and the Historians*, and in 1956 Ludwig von Mises developed a sustained analysis of *The Anti-Capitalistic Mentality*.[1] Whether there is a bias against capitalism in the humanities and social sciences is not subject to serious discussion. But its exact nature, causes, and consequences might usefully be explored, perhaps especially by humanists.

Speaking of the situation among German historians from 1850–1914, Hayek writes: "No reproach was more feared or more fatal to academic prospects than that of being an 'apologist' of the capitalist system; and, even if a scholar dared to contradict dominant opinion on a particular point, he would be careful to safeguard himself against such accusation by joining in the general condemnation of the capitalist system."[2]

Dr. Hacker adds an interesting point: "Generally, it may be said, one notes an anticapitalist bias. But in the United States, at any rate, the anticapitalist bias of many of its historians is not necessarily due to Marxist influences."[3] Dr. Hacker then cites several other influences, including certain forms of agrarianism as in the moral vision of Charles A. Beard, whose childhood in Indiana nourished a romantic critique of capitalism innocent of institutional, class, or economic

---

[1] Friedrich A. Hayek, ed., *Capitalism and the Historians* (Chicago: University of Chicago Press, 1954), and Ludwig von Mises, *The Anti-Capitalistic Mentality* (Van Nostrand: Libertarian Press, 1972).

[2] Hayek, *Capitalism and the Historians*, p. 23.

[3] Louis Hacker, "The Anticapitalist Bias of American Historians," ibid., p. 74.

analysis; and in the social democratic vision of Gustavus Myers, whose *History of the Great American Fortunes* (1909) influenced Mathew Josephson's *The Robber Barons* (1934). Writers like Beard and Myers, Hacker reports, established a classic non-Marxist way of condemning capitalism based upon such "attitudes" as these: "(1) that great fortunes in America were built up by fraud; (2) that the country's natural resources were looted in the process; and (3) that the social consequences of private ownership and wealth were unhappy—in creating classes, in subordinating agriculture, in building slums, etc."[4] Each of these assertions is empirically dubious; the attitudes behind them do not derive from empirical studies.

Bertrand de Jouvenel contributes to Hayek's volume one of the most brilliant analyses of the intelligentsia—that predecessor of the "new class" praised by John Kenneth Galbraith and criticized by Irving Kristol[5]—an acute analysis whose utility may be glimpsed in this passage:

> The intellectual's hostility to the businessman presents no mystery, as the two have, by function, wholly different standards, so that the businessman's normal conduct appears blameworthy if judged by the criteria valid for the intellectual's conduct. . . . The businessman offers to the public "goods" defined as anything the public will buy; the intellectual seeks to teach what is "good," and to him some of the goods offered are things of no value which the public should be discouraged from wanting. The world of business is to the intellectual one in which the values are wrong, the motivations low, the rewards misaddressed. A convenient gateway into the intellectual's inner courtyard where his judgments are rendered is afforded by his deficit preference. It has been observed that his sympathy goes to institutions which run at a loss, nationalized industries supported by the treasury, colleges dependent on grants and subsidies, newspapers which never get out of the red. Why is this? Because he knows from personal experience that, whenever he acts as he feels he should, there is unbalance between his effort and its reception: to put it in economic jargon, the market value of the intellectual's output is far below factor input. That is because a really good thing in the intellectual realm is a thing which can be recognized as good by only a few. As the intellectual's role is to make people know for true

---

[4] Ibid., p. 80.

[5] See H. Bruce-Biggs, *The New Class?* (New Brunswick, N.J.: Transaction Books, 1979).

and good what they did not previously recognize as such, he encounters a formidable sales resistance, and he works at a loss. When his success is easy and instantaneous, he knows it for an almost certain criterion that he has not truly performed his function. Reasoning from his experience, the intellectual suspects whatever yields a margin of profit of having been done, not from belief in and devotion to the thing, but because enough people could be found to desire it to make the venture profitable. You may plead with the intellectual and convince him that most things must be done this way. Still he will feel that those ways are not his. His profit-and-loss philosophy can be summed up in these terms: to him a loss is the natural outcome of devotion to a-thing-to-be-done, while a profit, on the other hand, is the natural outcome of deferring to the public.

The fundamental difference of attitude between the businessman and the intellectual can be pinned down by resort to a hackneyed formula. The businessman must say: "The customer is always right." The intellectual cannot entertain this notion. A bad writer is made by the very maxim which makes him a good businessman: "Give the public what it wants." The businessman operates within a framework of tastes, of value judgments, which the intellectual must ever seek to alter. The supreme activity of the intellectual is that of the missionary offering the Gospel to heathen nations.[6]

De Jouvenel states that intellectuals, committed to truth, are prone to take toward businessmen an attitude of moral superiority like that of the Pharisee toward the publican. He gently notes that the poor man lying by the wayside was lifted up by a merchant (the Samaritan) and not by the intellectual (the Levite). The intellectuals, he observes, are growing enormously in number but are losing their ability to compel obedience. They are caught in an "inferiority complex" brought on by reduced status in the marketplace of esteem. He suggests that the much-discussed status of the industrial wage earner may be a less serious class problem for a modern system than the status of the intellectuals.

Countless texts might be amassed from the humanities and the social sciences to illustrate the denigration of capitalism by intellectuals. In the humanities, one can think of few plays, novels, essays, or studies that do not reflect the contempt of the first protectors of the humanists, the aristocratic class, for the crass new

---

[6] Bertrand de Jouvenel, "The Treatment of Capitalism by Continental Historians," in Hayek, *Capitalism and the Historians*, pp. 116-18.

world of business, the bourgeois ethic, and the culture of profits and commerce. Almost every conceivable image of evil, or at least of ugliness, has been heaped upon bourgeois civilization. The liberal tradition, as Lionel Trilling has noted, constitutes in the modernist period "an adversary culture"—and what it is adversary to is the culture of democratic capitalism.

The humanist rarely studies the achievements of democratic capitalism in providing the material base for average longevity almost twice as high as that of previous eras, for unparalleled mobility and liberty, for educational opportunities and attainments, for health and self-government. The animus against capitalism is expressed in aesthetic, moral, and even in frankly nostalgic terms. It is sometimes also expressed in utopian terms, as though new economic systems bloomed like a thousand flowers, to be developed at will. It is difficult to think of significant humanists who have welcomed, evaluated, and defended democratic capitalism for its accomplishments, even while recognizing its limits, evils, and flaws.

In particular, it is difficult to find theologians who have created a theology of democratic capitalism. Virtually all the major theologians have declared themselves socialist: Tillich, Barth, Bonhoeffer, Moltmann, Niebuhr, Rauschenbusch. Despite Max Weber, one cannot find Calvinist theologians who welcomed democratic capitalism or discovered in it a Christian impulse. (Although one can find preachers, closer to the people, who did.) Scholars note in objection to Weber that in Geneva and in Scotland, two strongholds of Calvinism, the development of democratic capitalism was retarded, not advanced, by Calvinist conviction. Now all this is odd. Theologians do not hesitate to undertake a "development of doctrine" and to become up-to-date in their ethical and theological analyses. In the actual praxis of socialism since 1917 or even since 1945 (in more than half the nations of the world), it is empirically difficult to discern why socialism should commend itself to the Christian conscience and democratic capitalism should not. Are citizens less equal *in fact* in democratic capitalist societies than in socialist societies? Are they less free? Is there less community, free association, sociality, fraternity? Is intellect less fettered? Are inventiveness and creativity less in evidence? Is "alienation" greater? Such matters are subject to empirical testing.

There is no longer any excuse for merely dreaming about socialism. It is embodied in many nations, under many different circumstances. Its programs have been tried. Its record of achievement is open to inspection. Its contradictions—in praxis rather than in theory—have had time to appear. One would expect theologians to

57

be as neutral with respect to socialism as they are with respect to capitalism, but they are not. No extended empirical comparison has been conducted by a Christian theologian measuring the degree to which, in actual practice, democratic capitalism approximates at least some of the principles of the Gospels, as opposed to the degree by which the praxis of socialism does. Nor has any theologian tried to elicit from empirical reality the functioning *ideals* of democratic capitalism, so that these might be compared, ideal for ideal, with those of socialism.

For generations, socialism existed as an idea in books, without embodiment in any nation. Democratic capitalism, by contrast, developed without much benefit of theory or help from intellectuals. It was led by doers, not by thinkers, by producers of goods, not by humanists. So long as intellectuals were few and weak, the fact that democratic capitalism lacked intellectual self-consciousness offered no source of alarm. For generations, traditional conceptions (of justice, for example) on the part of theologians, aristocratic biases among humanists, and socialist biases among social scientists prevented any serious effort on the part of intellectuals anywhere to provide a theory and a vision for a system evolving well enough, but blindly, in practice. Socialist, aesthetic, and moral charges against democratic capitalism were seldom, if ever, replied to, and such charges were repeated incessantly. Few thinkers examined their accuracy. Few identified their own fate with that of democratic capitalism. They acted as though they were "outside" the system. Christians have been schooled to distrust and renounce "the world"; somehow, the capitalist "world" has been easier for Christian intellectuals to renounce than the socialist "world."

Dr. Norman's essay describes a state of facts, true for the intellectual class of Great Britain over several generations, and true as well for the intellectual climate of the United States. To argue in favor of a profit system is to oppose the weight of enlightened opinion. To argue in favor of corporations large enough to check, at least in part, the immense power of the central administrative state is not common. To embrace the principle of the (imperfect but effective) separation of the political order from the economic order is not to be in tune with the ideology of *Christianity and Crisis, The Commonweal, The Christian Century,* or of "enlightened" opinion elsewhere. Experiment and see. Hostility to profits, large corporations, and an independent private sector is quite tangible.

The denigration of capitalism so overwhelms us that the true state of affairs will at first seem, even to those who come to see it, perverse. Knowing what we know about the praxis of democratic capitalism and that of socialism, we may judge that the first is at least as close to the Gospels in its conceptions of the person, conscience, community, state, sin, creativity, liberty, and equality as is the second. Where economic liberty is weakened political liberty is weakened in due proportion. Since neither the state nor a set of economic institutions is to be trusted, to absorb one in the other is to concentrate power and to diminish liberty.

On the other hand, the theories of John Locke, Adam Smith, and John Stuart Mill are not adequate to explain the actual practice of democratic capitalism. The classic texts of such thinkers lack a sufficient sense of community, are too focused upon the individual, and employ too atomistic a method of analysis. Their theories about the family, the neighborhood, the labor union, the corporation, and other social institutions natural and voluntary, are not robust enough to explain how we actually live under democratic capitalism. Democratic capitalism does not entail—indeed it could not survive if it were dependent upon—materialism, individualism, or laissez faire. It is a political system, an economic system, and a cultural system, three in one, a trinity of autonomous but interdependent systems. It generates immense social activity, associations of every sort, teamwork, cooperation. It is, in practice, quite different from the picture presented by the anticapitalist myth.

The virtue of Dr. Norman's essay is that it prompts us to detect in ourselves unconscious tides of intellectual mythmaking. Our eyes have been averted from our real experience of democratic capitalism; our perceptions are suffused with false consciousness, false guilts, false judgments. If we are to awaken from the land of myth, to be shaken from a long slumber, every anticapitalist assertion needs to be questioned. It is not an improper use of intellect to examine the evidence on which each is based. In our sort of society, one is free to become a socialist or a democratic capitalist (or whatever other options may be available). Even if one assumes that a "mixed economy"—supported by holding both the capitalist and the socialist principles in tension—is the best practical arrangement, it is still the capitalist principle that receives less loving attention from the intellectual. Given the centuries-old denigration of capitalism, a hard look at the conventional wisdom is demanded by simple honesty.

The new frontier for theological reflection, surely, is concern for economic questions. Naiveté about economics will not much longer provide evidence of serious purpose. What are the economic effects of socialist programs? Does socialism consist of practical programs, or is it only the name for a sort of "regulative ideal" of equality, fraternity, and the diminishment of alienation? As one tries to make up one's mind how to help shape public policy, one must ask: Is the praxis of socialism consonant with the predictions made by the theory of socialism? Are socialist ideals properly to be used as criteria for the praxis of democratic capitalism? Are there ideals implicit in the praxis of democratic capitalism that are more cogent than the ideals of socialism?

For example, it is now conceded by practicing socialists that not much is left of early optimism about socialist programs.[7] (1) The nationalization of industries has proved not to have the economic, political, or moral benefits once predicted for it. (2) Severe taxes on income and wealth in the name of distribution have not generated either the equal wealth or the moral benefits predicted; and the role of differential incentives has proved to be far more important to personal satisfaction and national wealth than was imagined. (3) Workers' control of the workplace has proved to be neither economically nor morally satisfactory; expert management is not as dispensable as had been imagined. (4) The social utility of wealth—in the building of parks, works of beauty, restaurants, experimentation in new technologies (like automobiles, television, calculators, and other devices made first for the wealthy, before going into mass production) —is higher than had been thought. (5) The sense of personal well-being that comes from entrepreneurial risk—on the part of blue-collar craftsmen, doctors, writers, actors, and many others—is far greater than socialist theory had projected. In a word, socialist programs are far more psychically destructive of liberty, work habits, élan, and personal accomplishment than ideology had anticipated.

Many theologians—permit me to cite the survey of political expectations for the 1980s published by The Commonweal (May 25, 1979)—speak glibly of redistribution, restraint of multinational corporations, and a "hidden majority" for socialism in the United States. There is a conspicuous silence about production and productivity, about incentives, and about the social utility of the unequal distribution of wealth. Theologians come late to such questions. One may hope that they do not fall victims to cant, whether socialist or capitalist. Their critical intelligence will need to operate in three directions at once.

---

[7] One may consult Leszek Kolakowski and Stuart Hampshire, The Socialist Idea (New York: Basic Books, 1974), and Anthony Crosland, "Socialism and the Private Sector," Dialogue, vol. 12 (1979), pp. 30-36. See also, Colin Welsh, "Crosland Reconsidered," Encounter, vol. 52 (1979), pp. 83-95.

Conventionally, economists concentrate rather too narrowly on the economic system, political scientists rather too narrowly on the political system; humanists have not done nearly all they ought upon the cultural system, which regulates and gives significance to economic and political activity. Democratic capitalism is a triune system; each person within it is governed by economic, political, and cultural practices. The system of democratic capitalism must be looked at as a whole. Theologians have an important role to play in analyzing this whole.

I would especially call attention to the tendency of socialist ways of thinking to reduce all three systems to a unitary system of "public" control. The word "public" is made to seem idealized, democratic, virtuous, selfless, and the word "private" is made to appear to be the source of selfishness, greed, and corruption. An empirical examination of public institutions and behaviors does not sustain such rosy hopes, nor does an empirical examination of private institutions or behaviors confirm such suspicions. It would be a useful task to estimate more exactly what our expectations of the public and private spheres ought realistically to be.

Further, there is a tendency for those under the spell of socialism to hold that our political freedoms will remain intact even if we alter our economic system quite profoundly. Indeed, hiding behind euphemism, Tom Hayden and Jane Fonda already speak of "economic democracy." In actual practice, the extension of public power over economic matters substantially enlarges public bureaucracies. Such extended power diminishes freedom of action, not only on the part of small entrepreneurs and large corporations, but also on the part of every economic agent, including workers. The same institutions in which political power is already vested will now acquire economic power as well. This concentration of power may appear to some to be benign. To others, it will signify a diminishment of creative liberties in an entire sector of life that earlier had been relatively free from state power. It may also signify a diminishment of the role of imagination, invention, discovery, and productivity throughout society. It may thus constitute a regression.

The principle of the separation of the economic system from the political system deserves close and practical attention. It does not entail laissez faire. But it does entail due regard for an excessive concentration of power in the state. This principle checks the socialist principle, which helped to effect our present "mixed economy" by abridging an excessive concentration of power in the private sector. A belated recognition of this dual principle prompted the recent conversion of Paul Johnson, former editor of *The New States-man*, from socialism to democratic capitalism.[8] Abandonment of this principle—especially through intellectual carelessness—would have serious effects upon the nature of our liberties. It is a critical issue for theological reflection. Dr. Norman deserves credit for urging us to think in a less prejudiced way about the system in which we live. That is only a step, but a necessary step, to the further task of pursuing the questions raised by Professors Marty, Schall, Cooke, and Burrell. It is one thing to denigrate democratic capitalism, another to attempt to understand it—but yet a third to create a nonsocialist and wholly apposite intellectual horizon within which to criticize it and to propel it forward toward all it can yet become.

---

[8] See Johnson's seminal essay, with responses, in Ernest W. Lefever, ed., *Will Capitalism Survive? A Symposium* (Washington, D.C.: Ethics and Public Policy Center, 1979).

CONTRIBUTORS

DAVID B. BURRELL, C.S.C., is professor of philosophy and chairman of theology at the University of Notre Dame and helped to initiate a University Committee on Education for Justice, which coordinates teaching, research, and related activities at the University. He is the author of *Exercises in Religious Understanding*.

BERNARD COOKE is professor of religious studies at the University of Calgary, Calgary, Alberta. He is the author of several books, the most recent being *Ministry to Word and Sacraments*, and is a frequent lecturer on religious studies. His professional interests have focused on christology and on the interaction of societal and Christian symbol systems.

MARTIN E. MARTY is the Fairfax M. Cone Distinguished Service Professor of the History of Modern Christianity at The University of Chicago and associate editor of *The Christian Century*. Among other works, he is the author of *A Nation of Behavers* and *Righteous Empire*, which won a National Book Award.

THE REV. DR. EDWARD R. NORMAN, a priest of the Anglican Church and assistant chaplain of Addenbrooke's Hospital, has been Dean of Peterhouse, Cambridge, since 1971. His doctorate, *The Catholic Church and Ireland* (1965), was followed by several books on Victorian England and Ireland and by *Church and Society in England, 1770–1970*.

The present lecture was commissioned by the Standing Conference of Employers of Graduates and delivered in 1977 at the Shell Centre in London.

MICHAEL NOVAK, now a resident scholar at the American Enterprise Institute, was formerly the Ledden-Watson Distinguished Professor of

Religion at Syracuse University. He has also taught at Harvard, Stanford, and The State University of New York at Old Westbury. His *American Vision: The Future of Democratic Capitalism* is another AEI publication in this series.

JAMES V. SCHALL, S.J., is associate professor, department of government, at Georgetown University. He has published articles in American and European journals and several books, including *Redeeming the Time, The Sixth Paul, Far Too Easily Pleased: A Theology of Play, Contemplation and Festivity,* and *The Praise of 'Sons of Bitches': On the Worship of God by Fallen Man.*